BOTANICALS

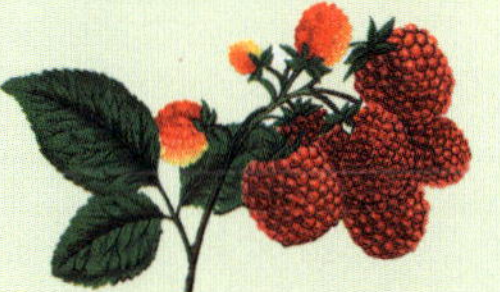

Cut & Collage

BOTANICALS

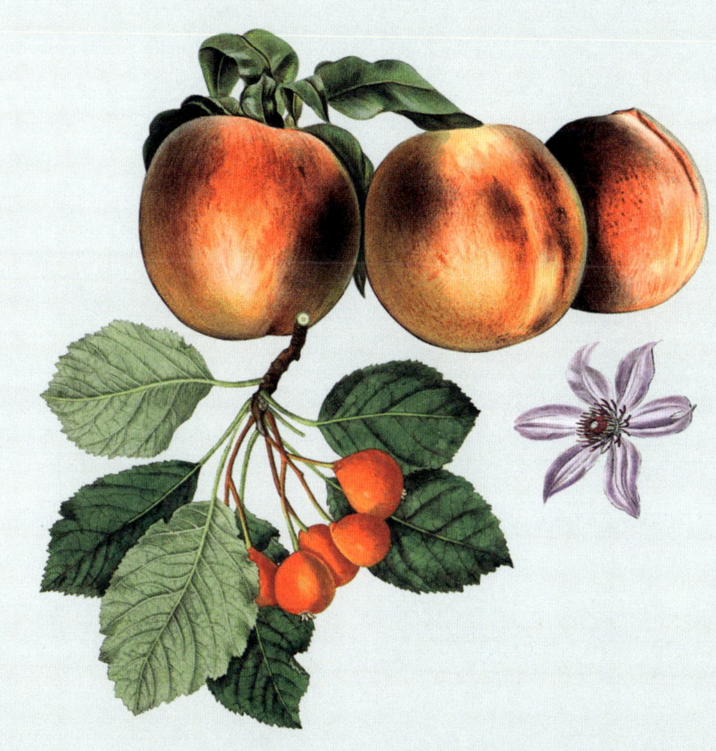

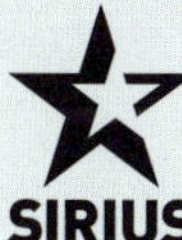

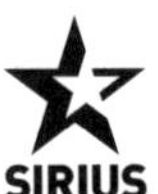

This edition published in 2025 by Sirius Publishing, a division of Arcturus Publishing Limited,
26/27 Bickels Yard, 151–153 Bermondsey Street,
London SE1 3HA

Copyright © Arcturus Holdings Limited

All rights reserved. No part of this publication may be reproduced, stored in a retrieval system, or transmitted, in any form or by any means, electronic, mechanical, photocopying, recording or otherwise, without prior written permission in accordance with the provisions of the Copyright Act 1956 (as amended). Any person or persons who do any unauthorised act in relation to this publication may be liable to criminal prosecution and civil claims for damages.

ISBN: 978-1-3988-5788-9
AD012980NT

Printed in China

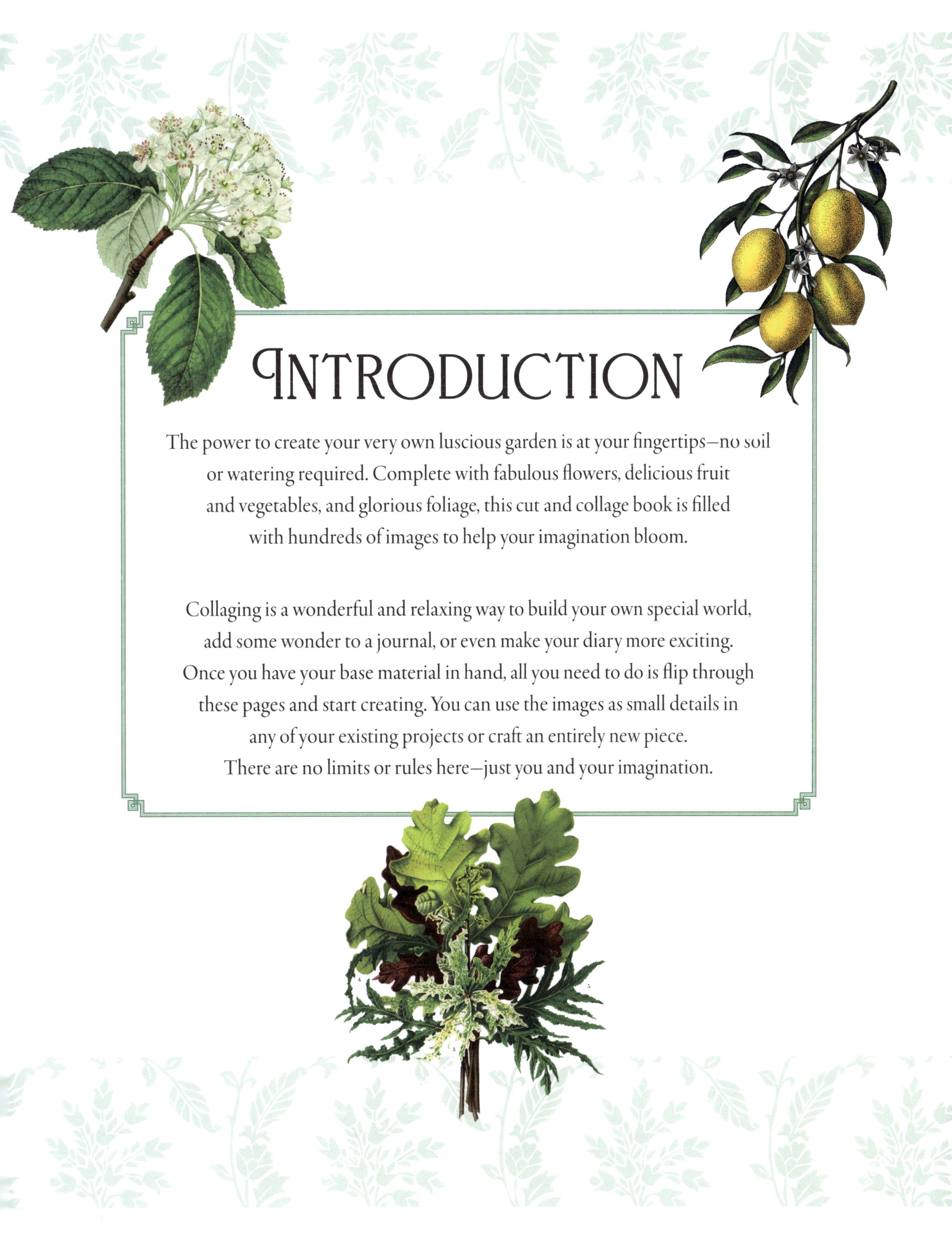

Introduction

The power to create your very own luscious garden is at your fingertips—no soil or watering required. Complete with fabulous flowers, delicious fruit and vegetables, and glorious foliage, this cut and collage book is filled with hundreds of images to help your imagination bloom.

Collaging is a wonderful and relaxing way to build your own special world, add some wonder to a journal, or even make your diary more exciting. Once you have your base material in hand, all you need to do is flip through these pages and start creating. You can use the images as small details in any of your existing projects or craft an entirely new piece. There are no limits or rules here—just you and your imagination.

Materials needed for collage:

Base material

A sheet of paper, a canvas, journal, or any other flat material will do. The thicker the paper, the easier it will be to layer your images.

Glue or tape

A glue stick, clear-dry liquid craft glue, or double-sided tape will keep your images in place.

Scissors

Any pair of scissors will suffice to cut out the images, but a hobby knife might be needed for more precision.

Additional materials for decoupage:

Decorative object

Use something like a pot plant, dish, or other decorative object as the base for your project.

Top coat

A varnish or lacquer is needed to ensure smoothness and preserve the integrity of your piece.

Paintbrush

A brush is needed to apply your top coat evenly. Additionally, it might be useful to use a brush and a liquid glue to secure your images for decoupage.

How to Collage

1.

With your base material ready to go, it's time to start collaging. Flip through the book until you find an image that speaks to you—it's best to start with a bigger one to build on. Using your scissors or hobby knife, carefully cut out the image and position it on the base. Reposition it as needed until you're happy with how it looks, then glue or tape it down.

2.

Once you have your first piece secured, it's time to start building around it. You can cut out your images all at once or one at a time, depending on your vision. Try to vary the size and look of your images as you go along. Part of the fun is making it as unique as possible.

3.

With your next piece(s) ready, start expanding your image. Layers are crucial in collaging as they add interest and depth to the project, so don't be afraid to get creative with it. Make dynamic scenes in front of historic landmarks or create your own vintage postcard—let the images guide you.

4.

If you're new to the art, try arranging all of the collected images without adhesive until you're happy with their placement—if they're glued down, it's hard to make any tweaks or changes. If you have other items handy, such as newspaper clippings or magazine images, you can add these to your piece as well for a varied, textured look.

5.

Once your collage feels complete, secure all the images with your adhesive and proudly display your art.

6.

These images can be used for a myriad of projects, not just collage.

7.

If you're working on a decoupage piece, repeat the process on a decorative object—a vase, a dish, or a piece of furniture—instead of a flat base material. Once you've set your images, go over your work with a lacquer or varnish to ensure that everything is evenly textured and properly sealed.

8.

For scrapbooking, use the images as details around your pictures to add a touch of whimsy to your memories.

Collage big or small - as long as you're having fun and letting your imagination be your guide.

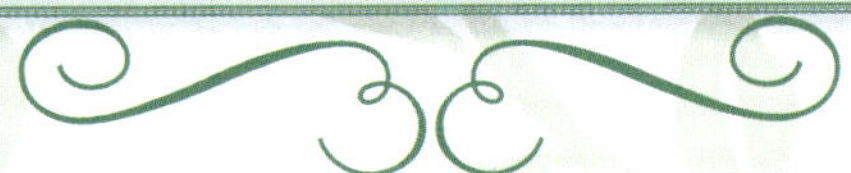

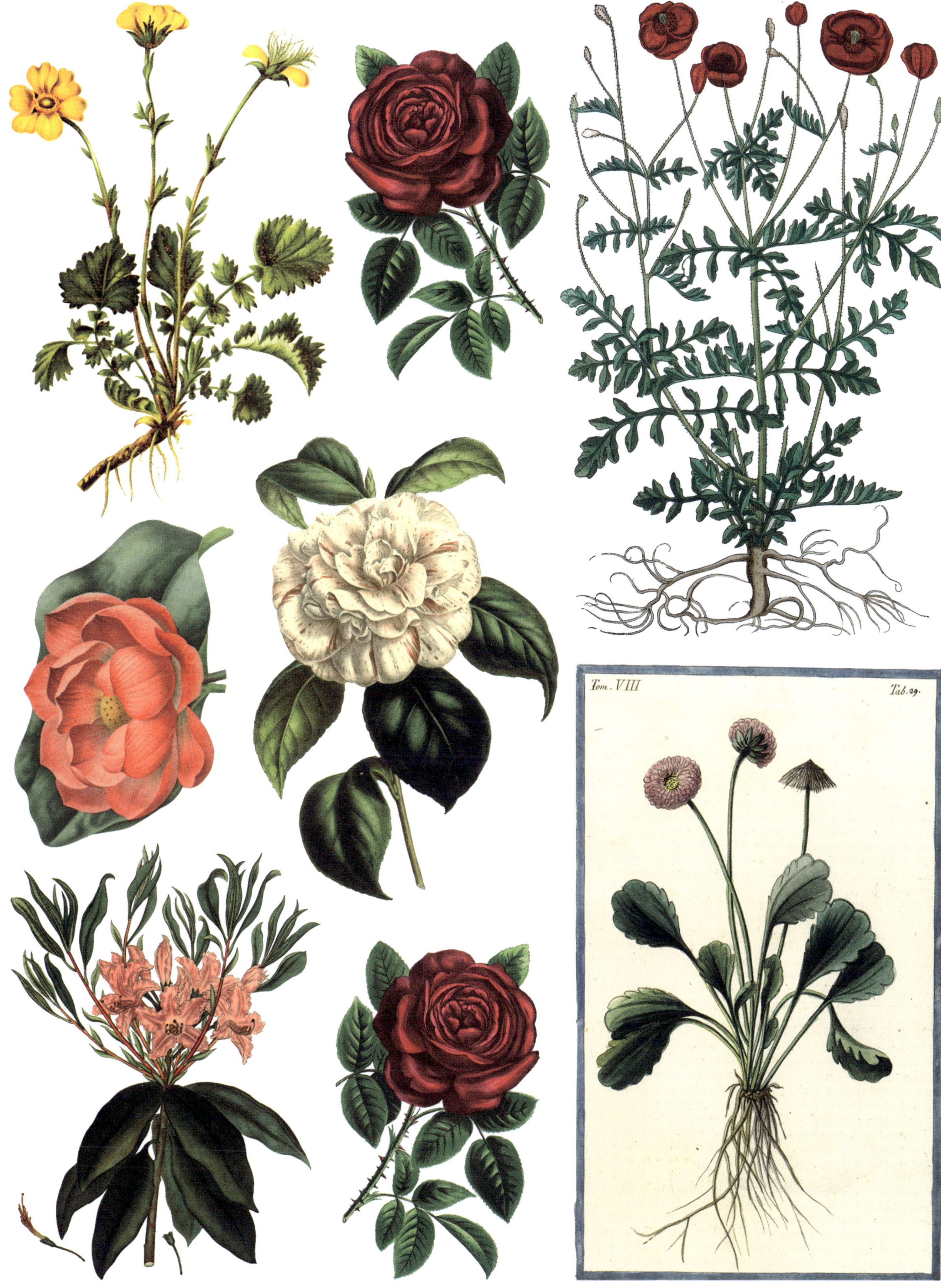
Tom. VIII
Tab. 29.

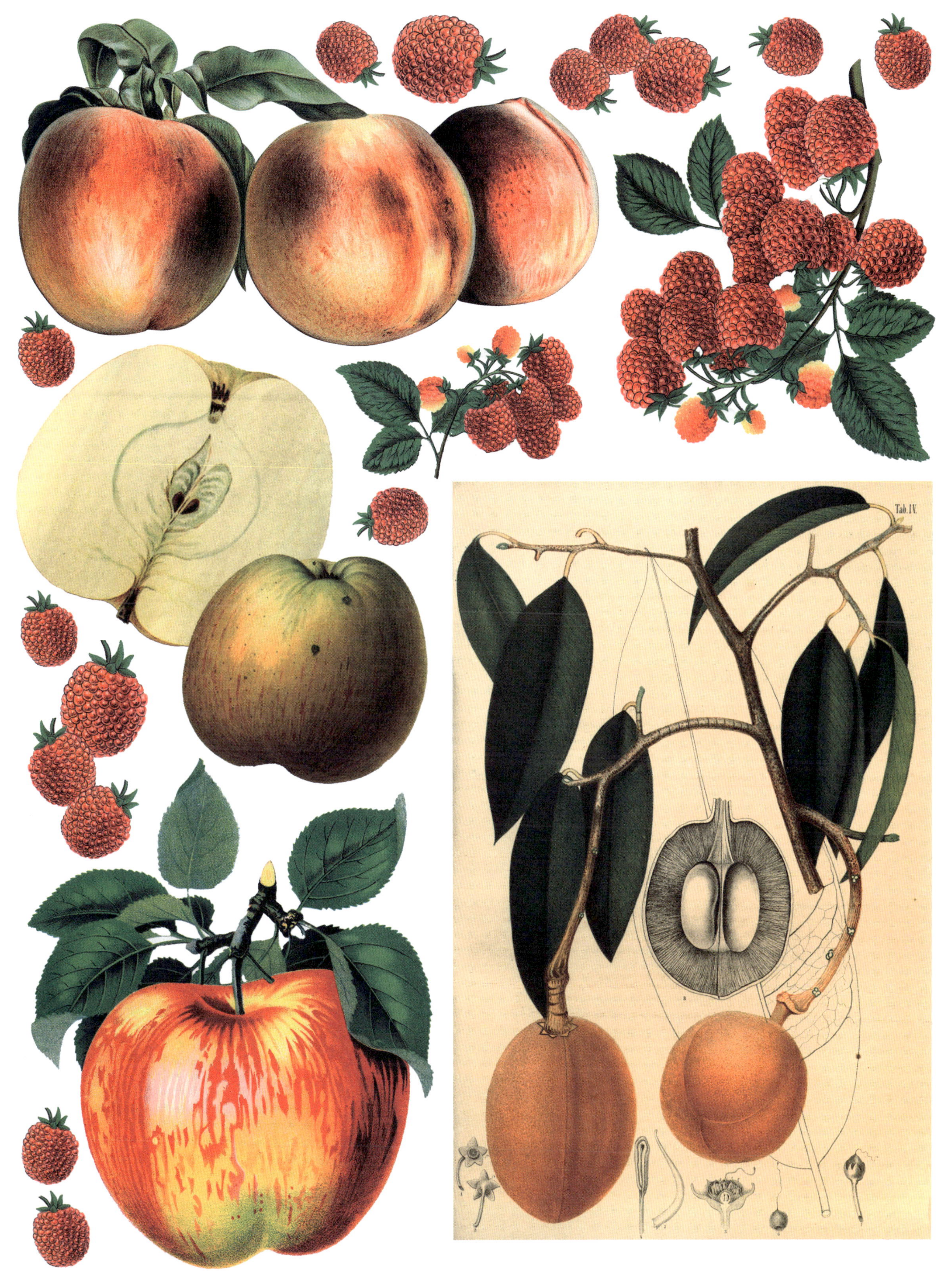
Tab. IV.

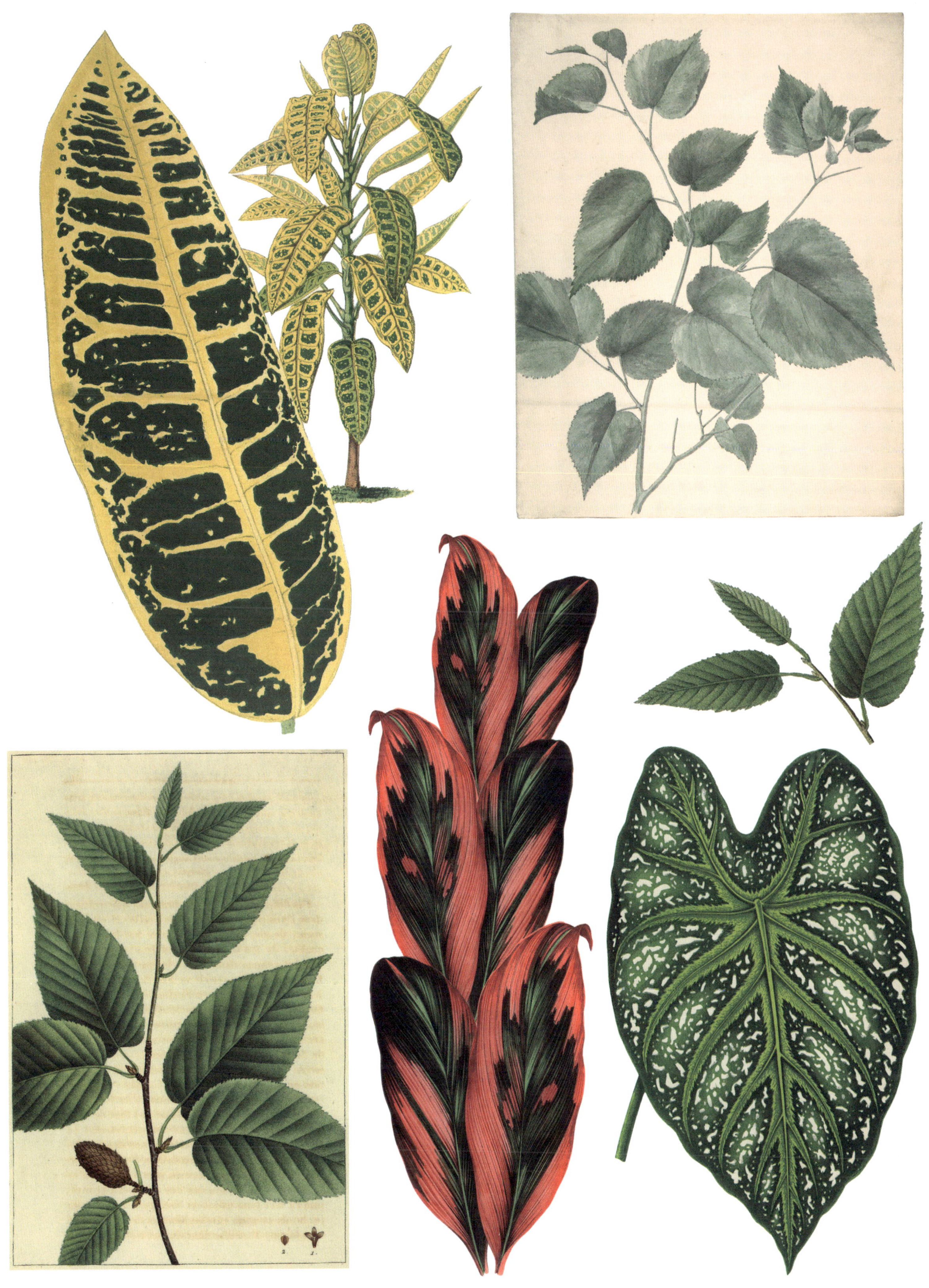

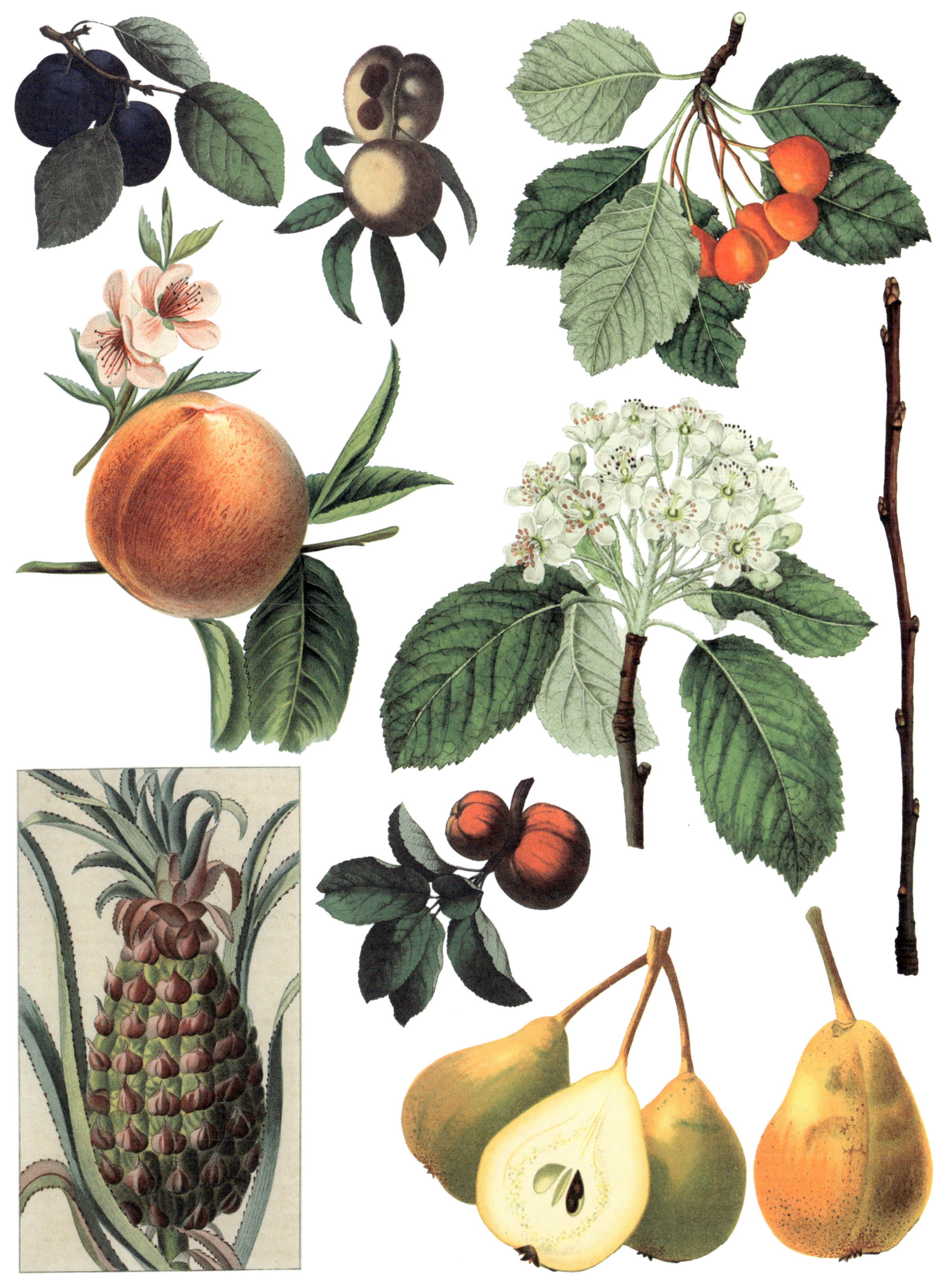

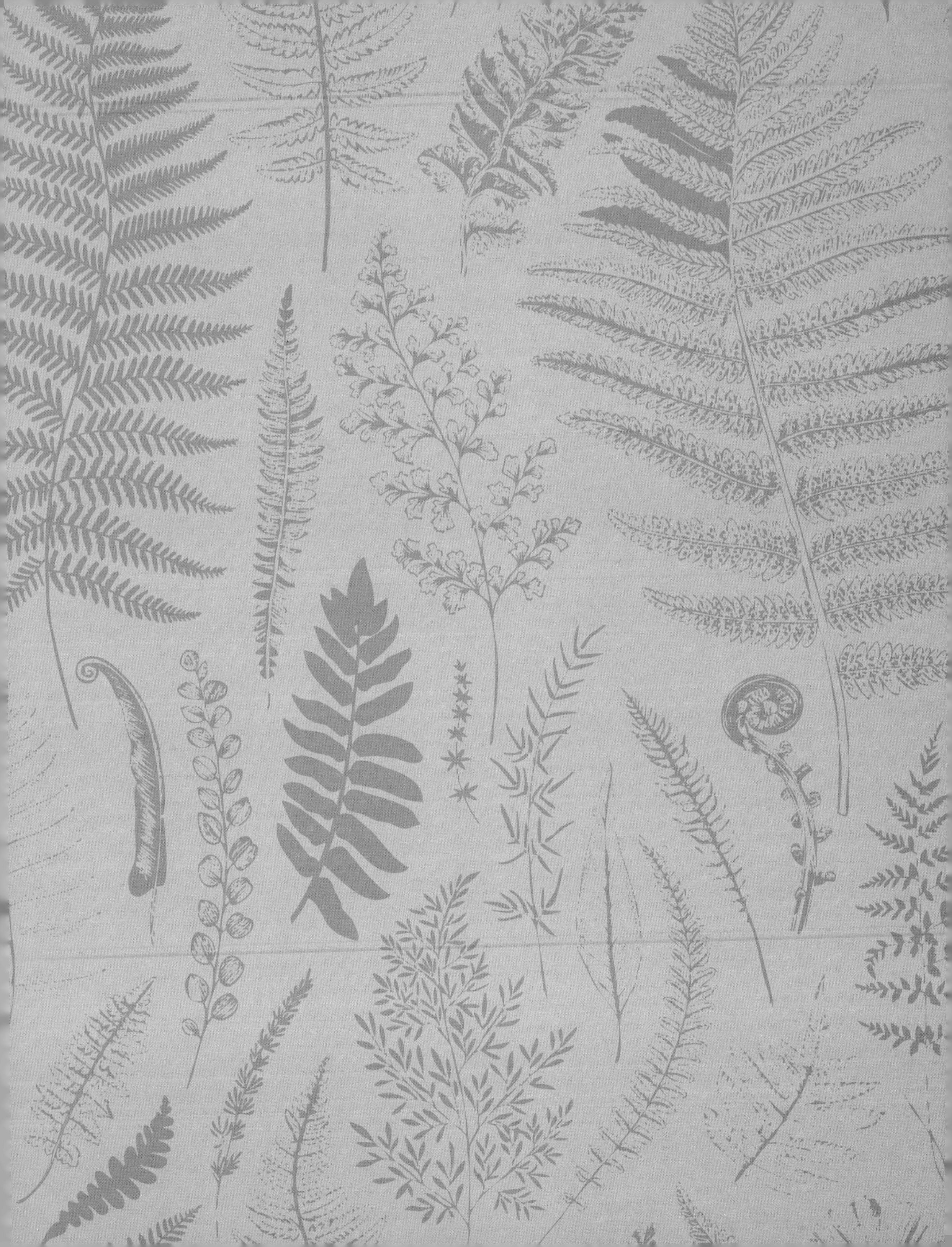

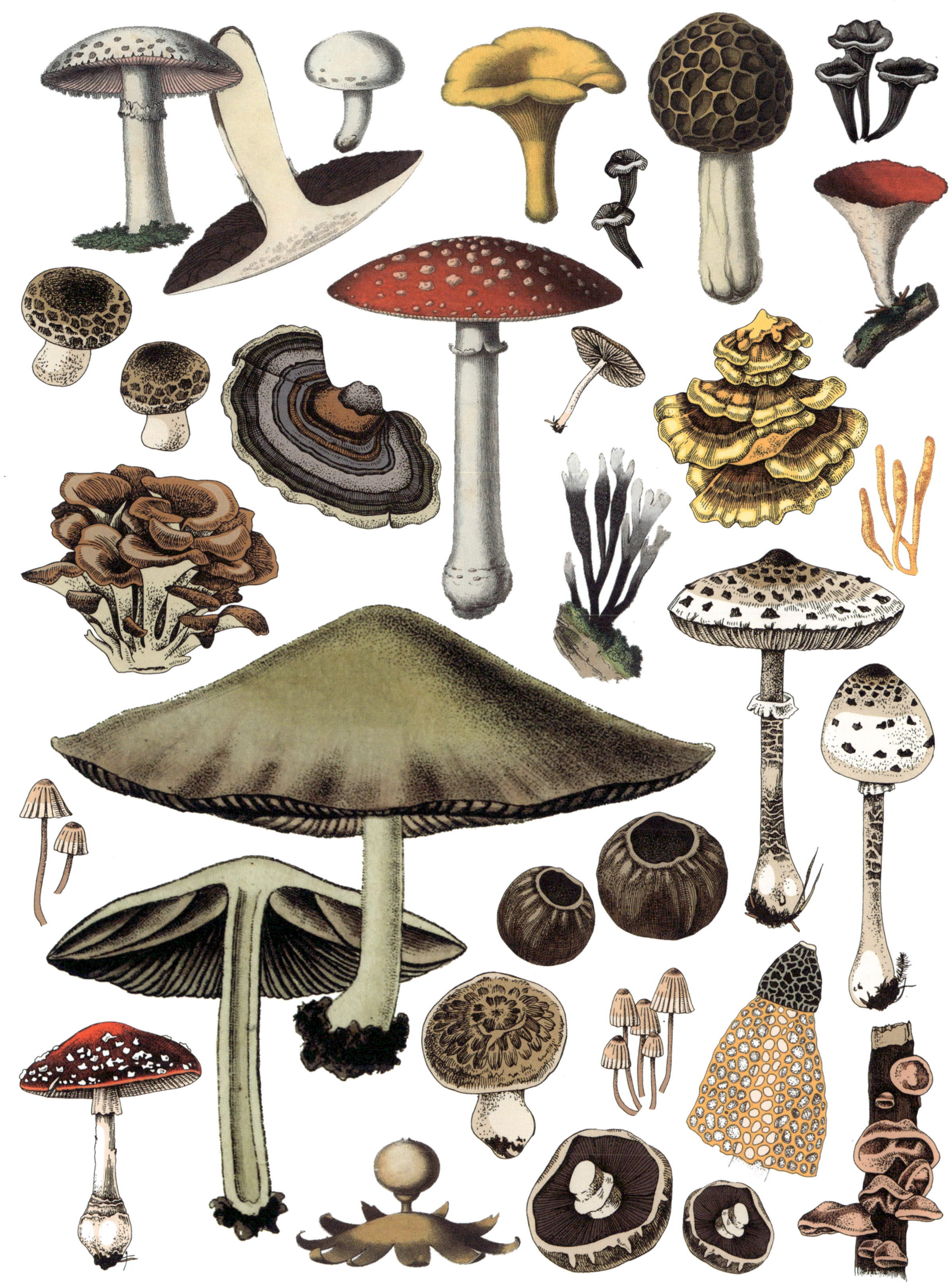

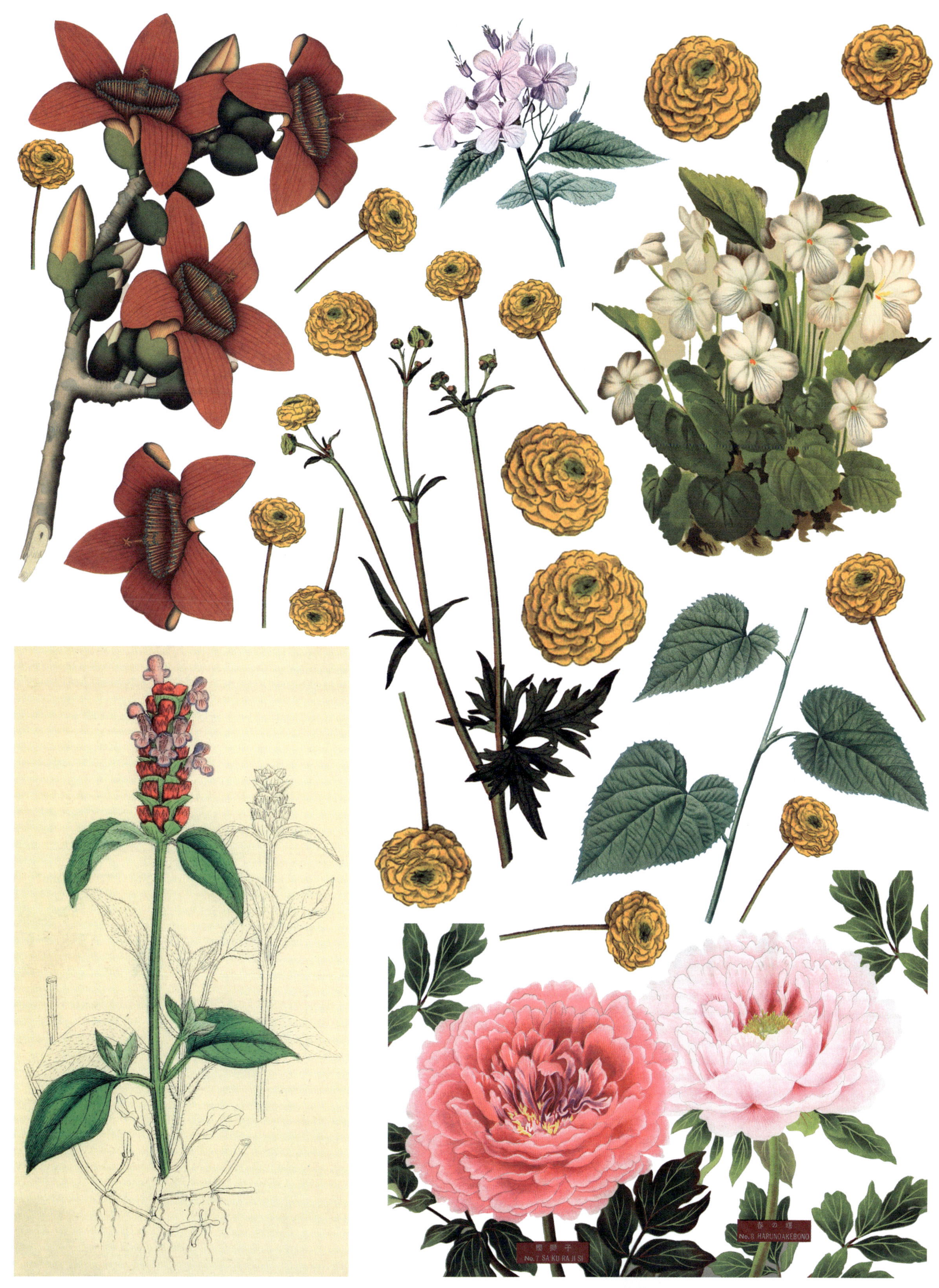
櫻獅子
No.7 SA KU RA JI SI
春の曙
No.8 HARUNOAKEBONO

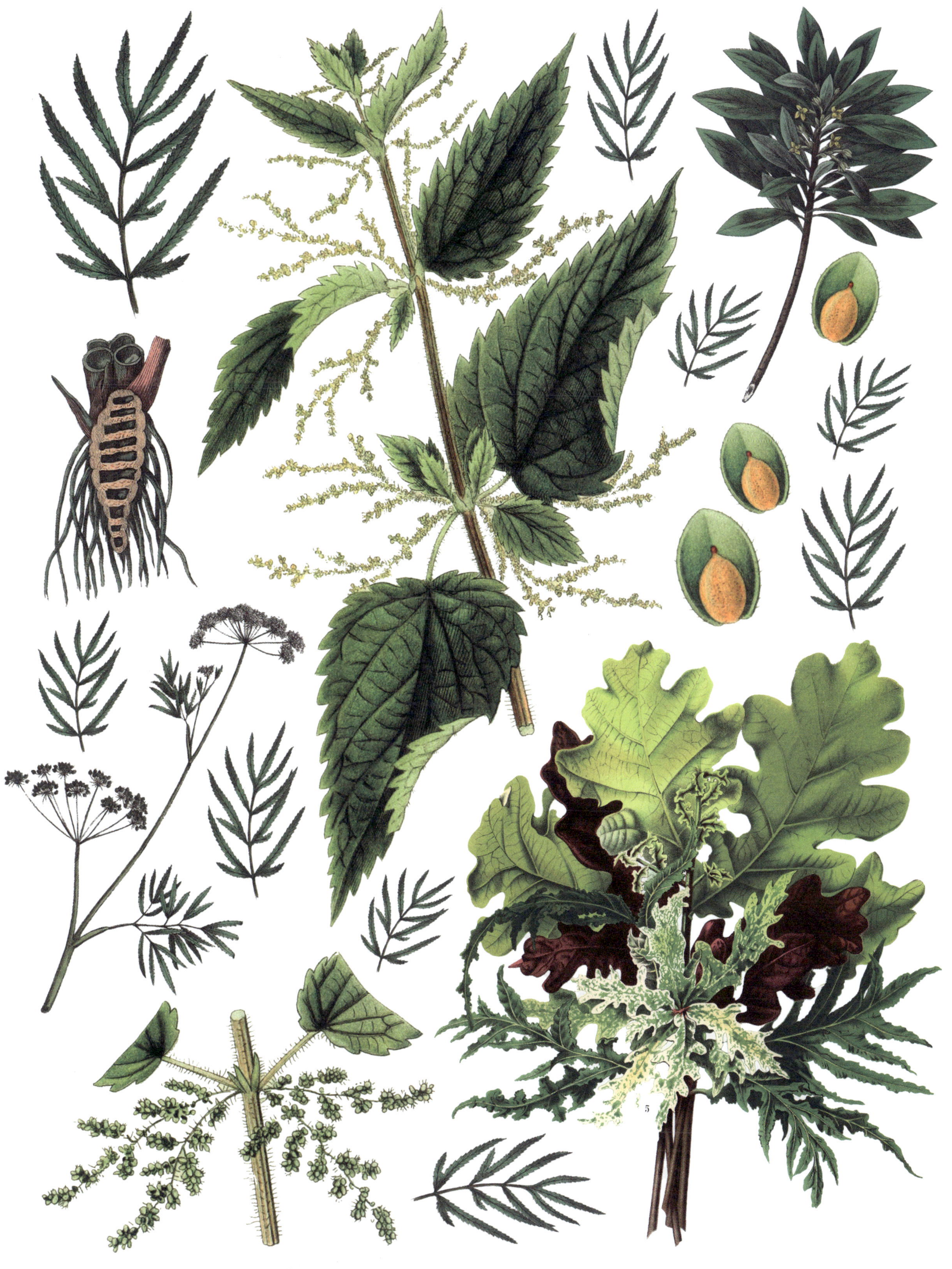
5

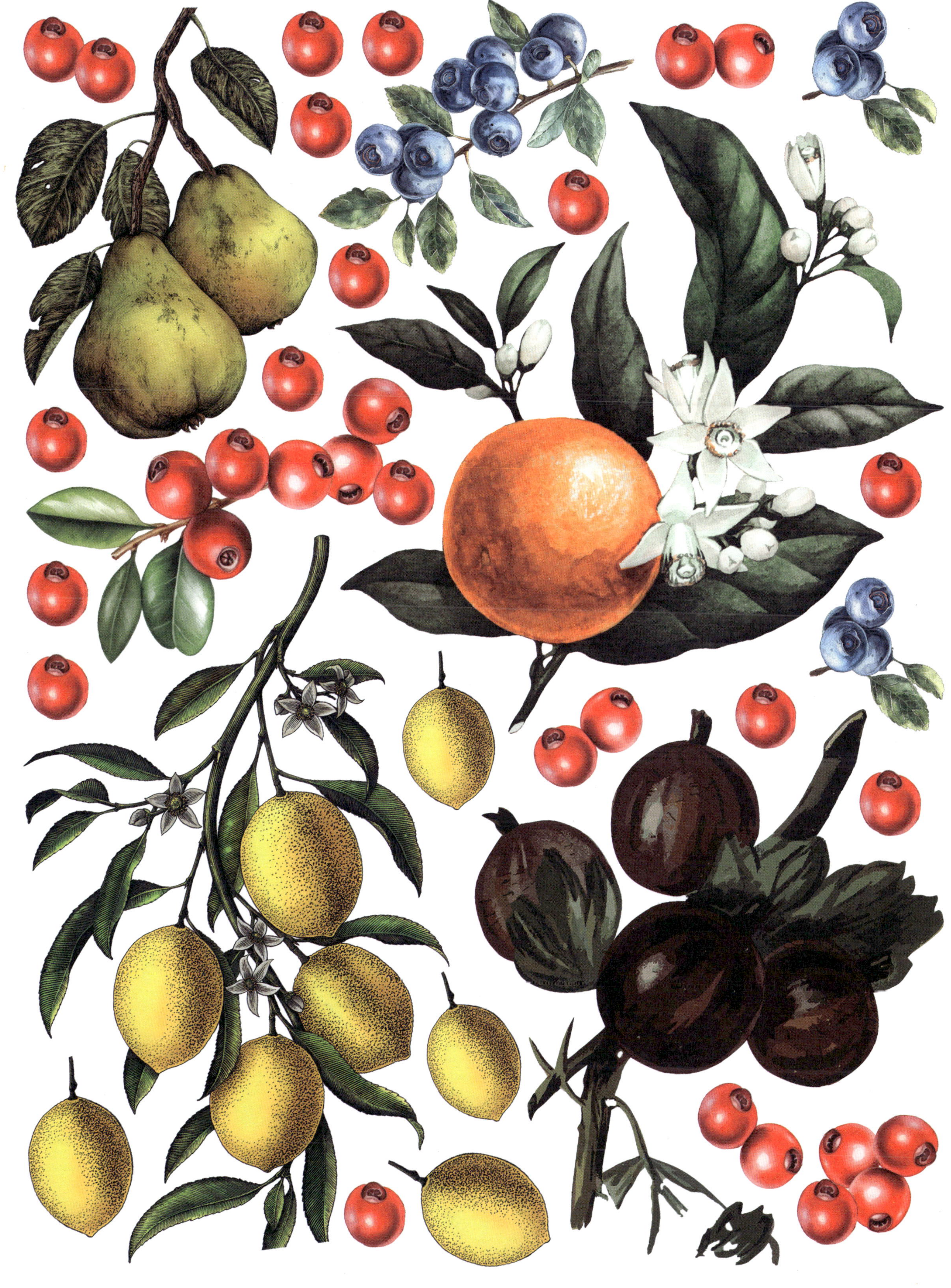

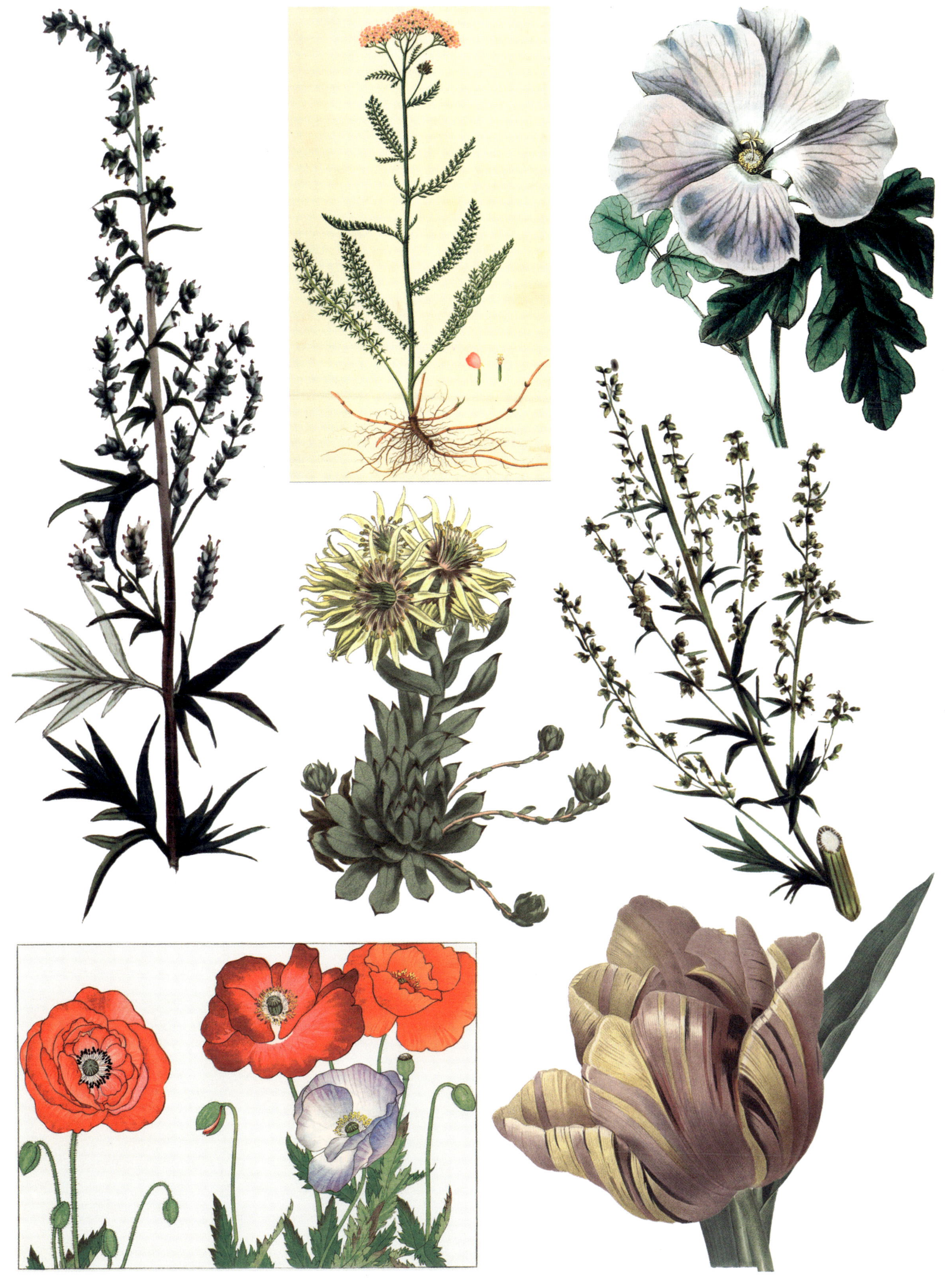

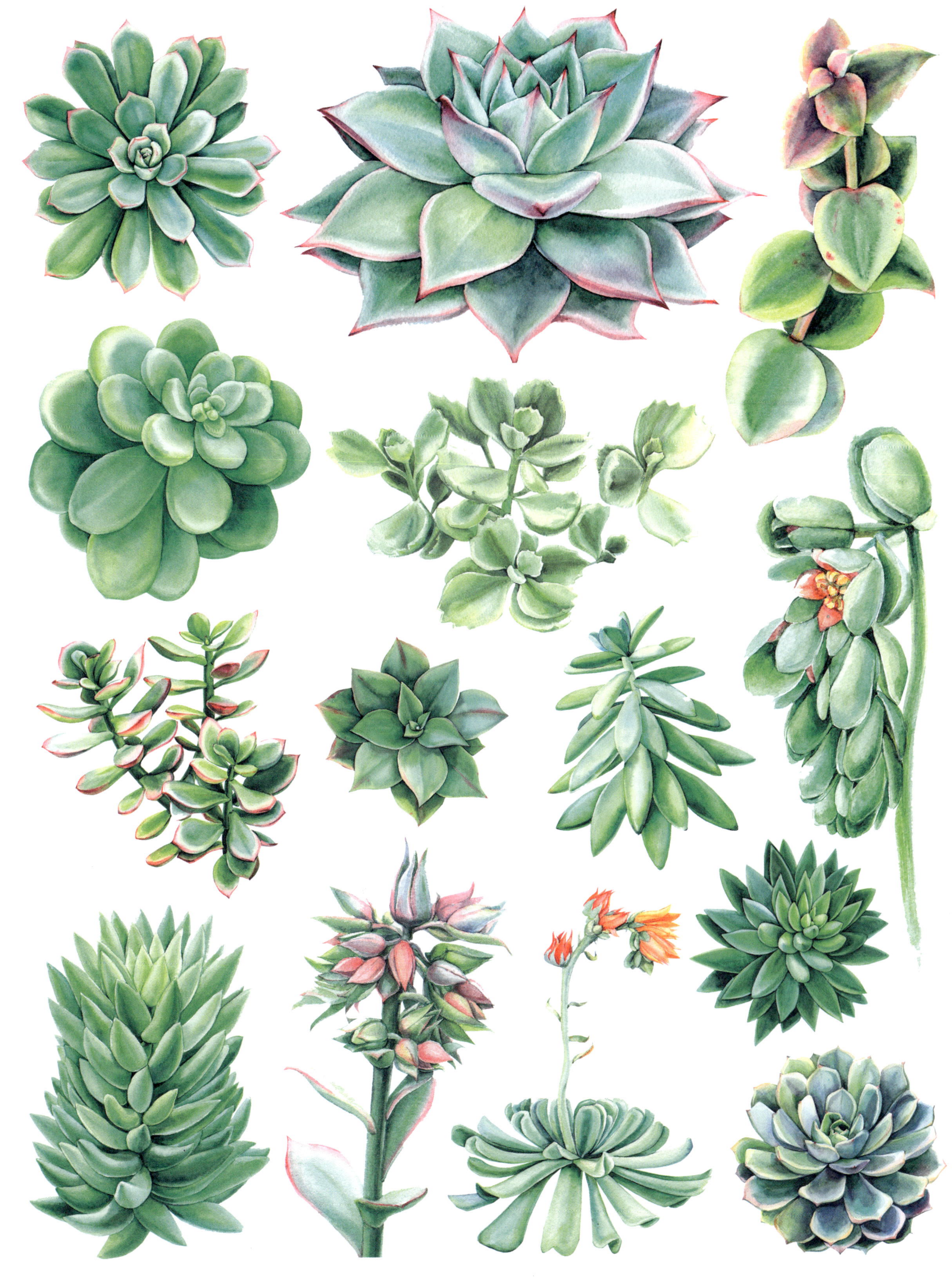

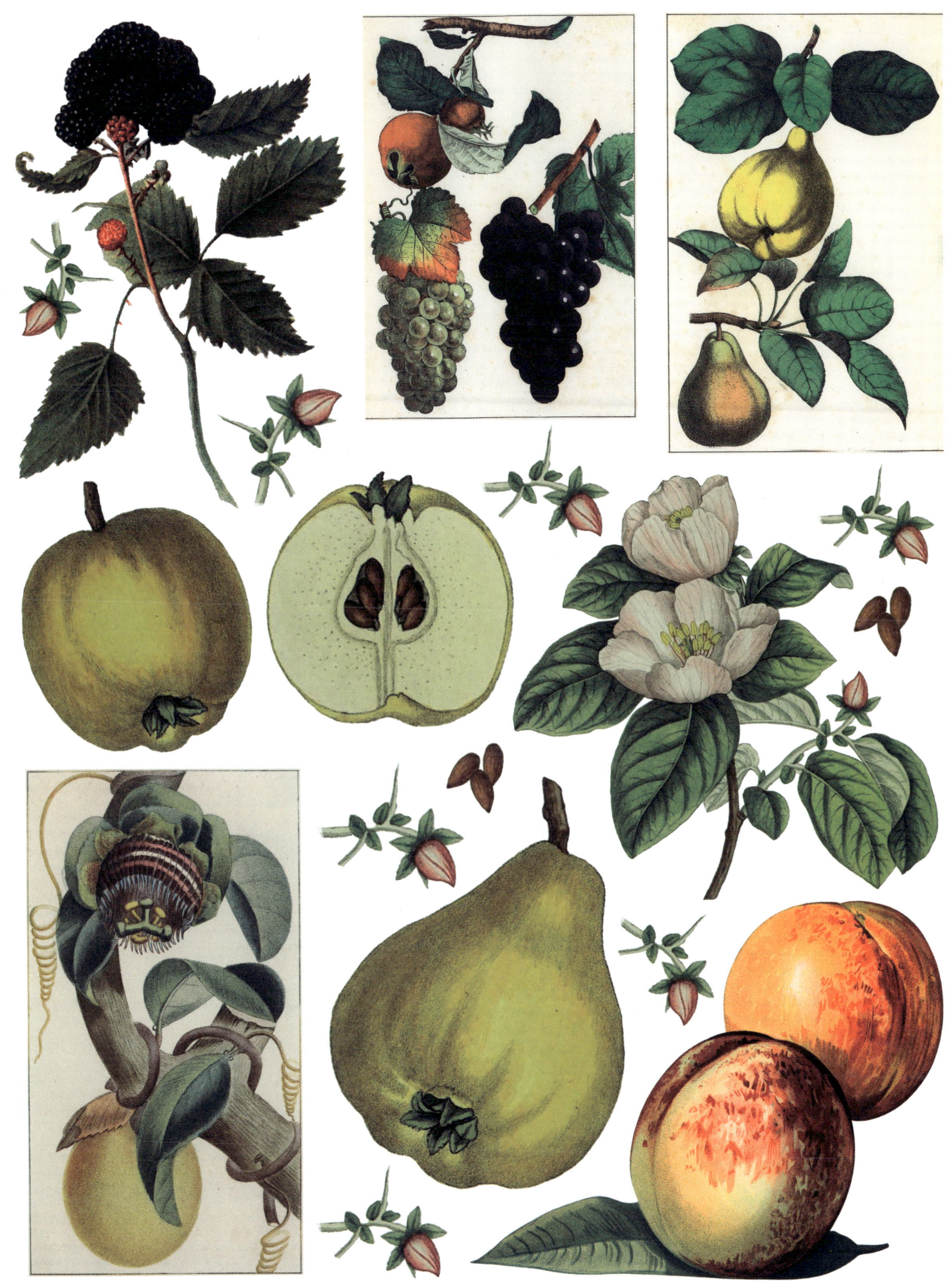

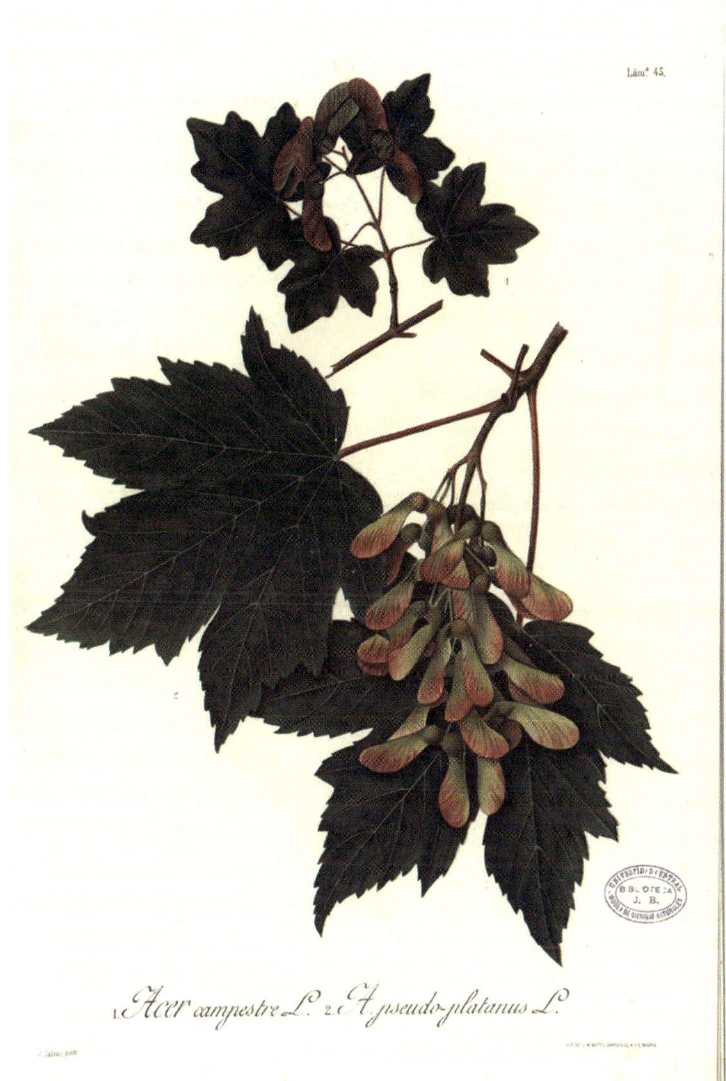
Lámᵃ 45.
1. Acer campestre L. 2. A. pseudo-platanus L.

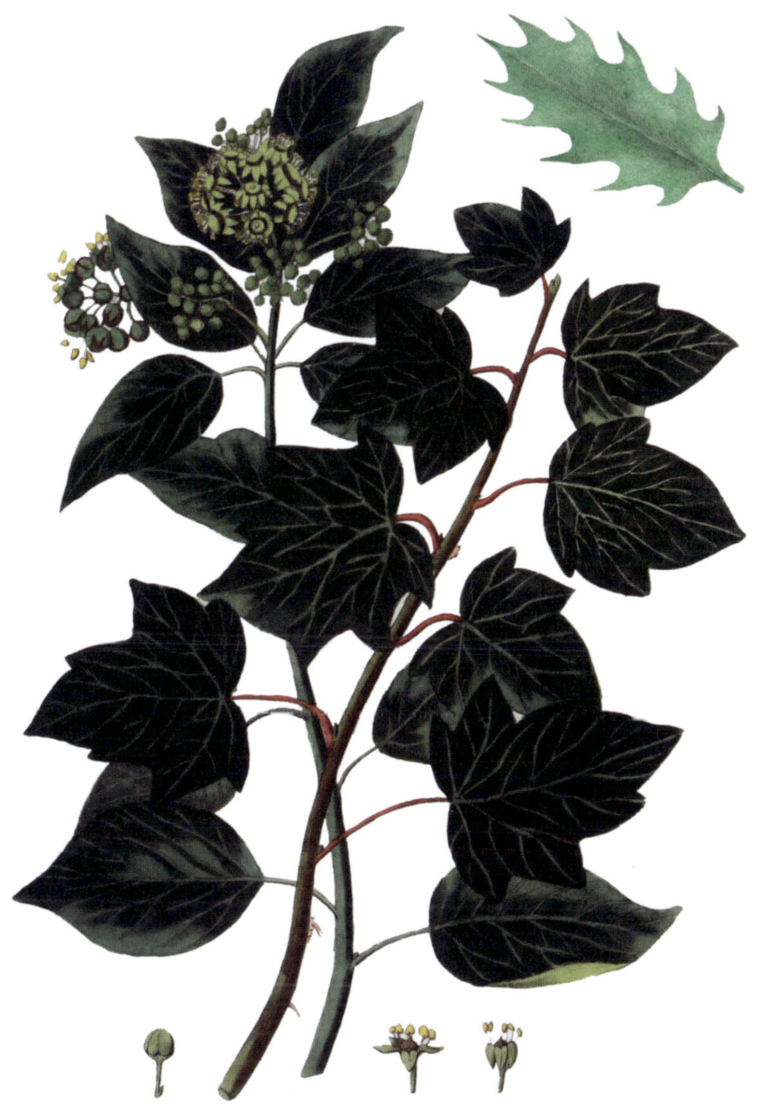

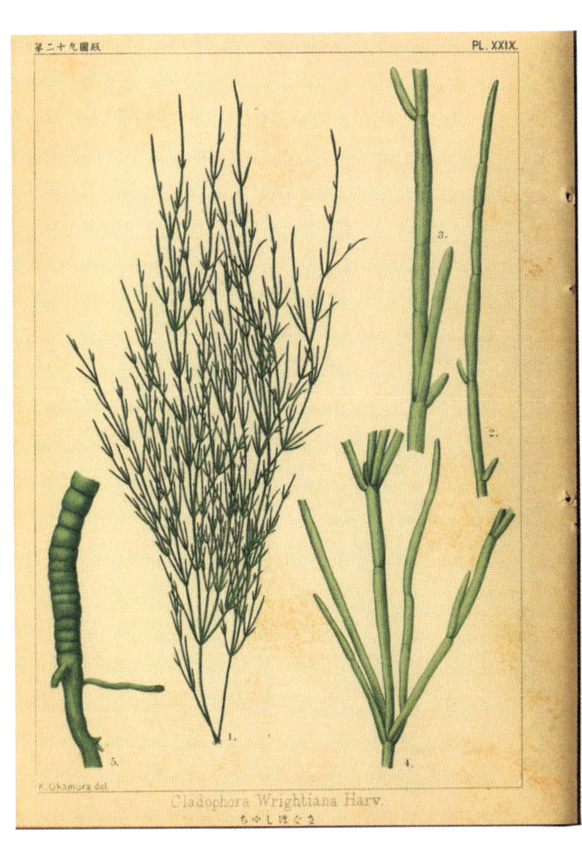
第二十九圖版
PL. XXIX.
K. Okamura del.
Cladophora Wrightiana Harv.

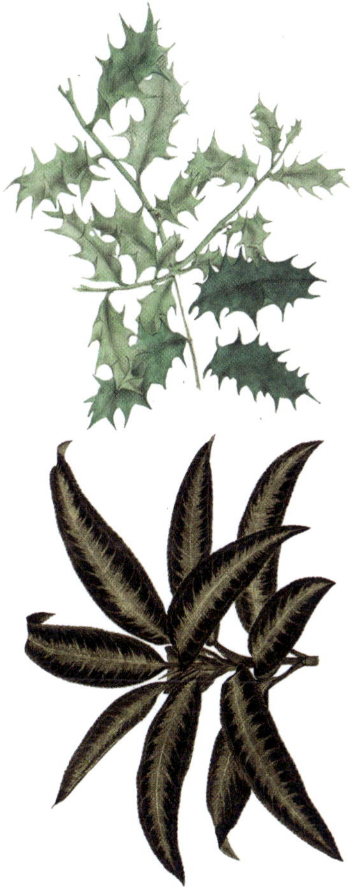

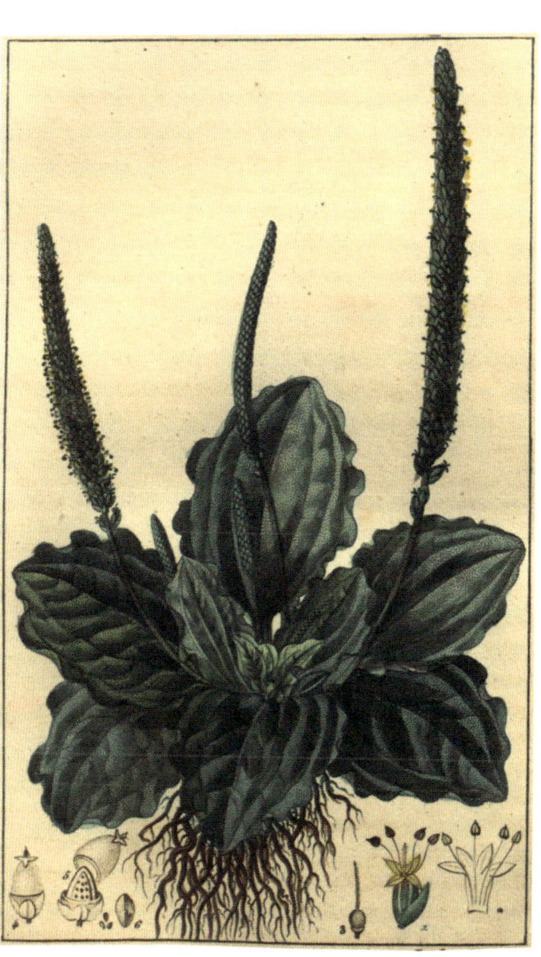

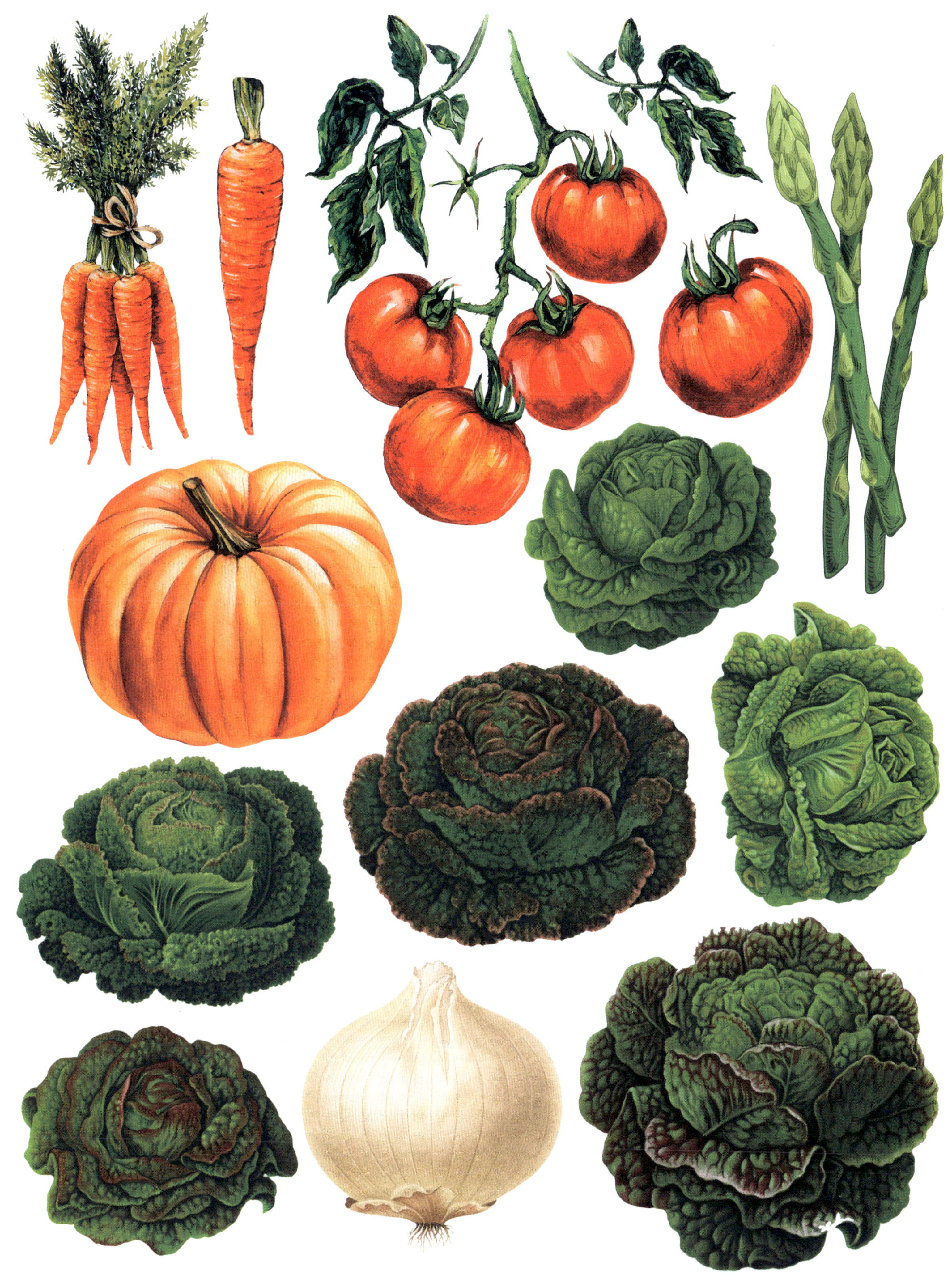

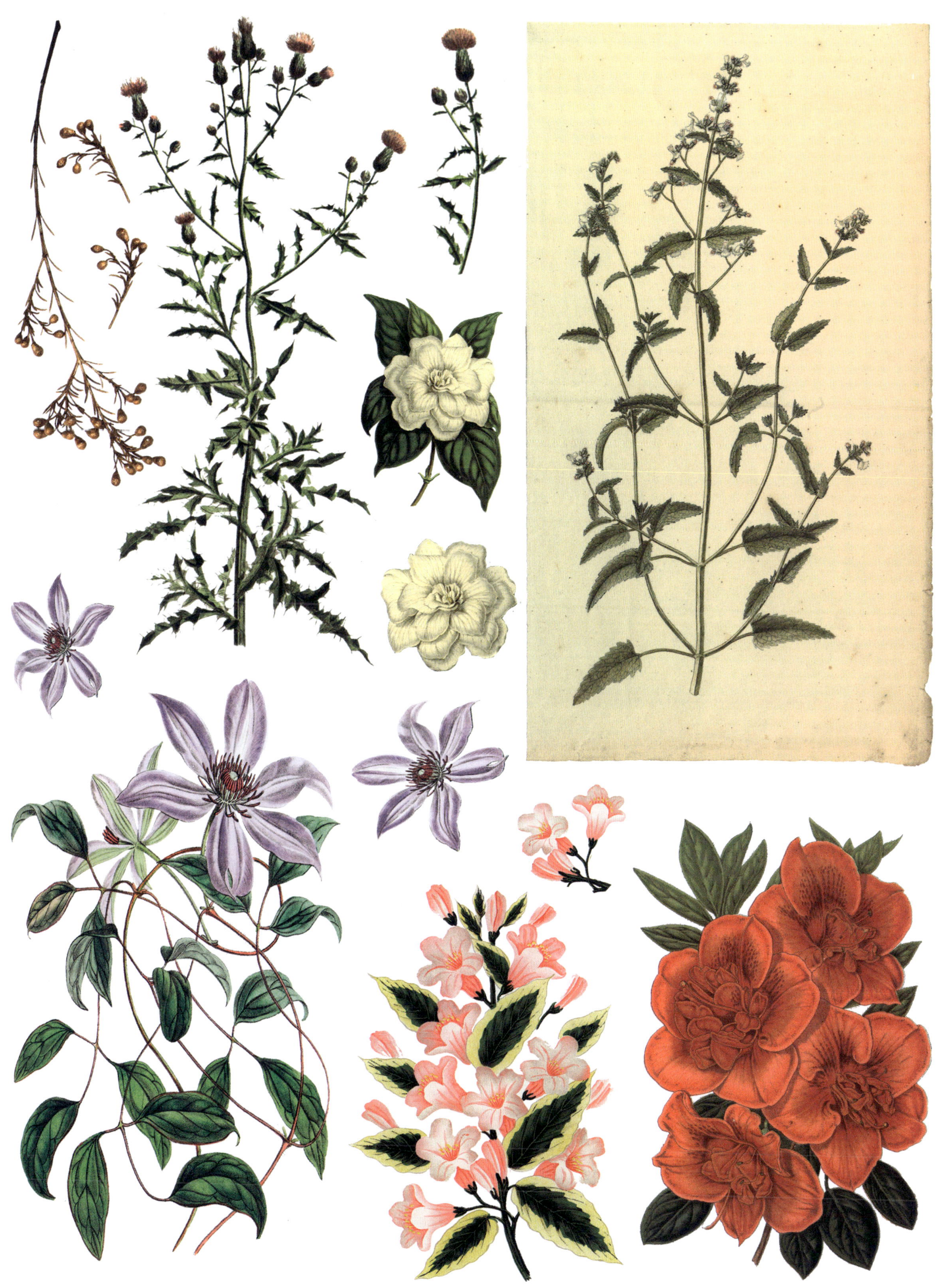

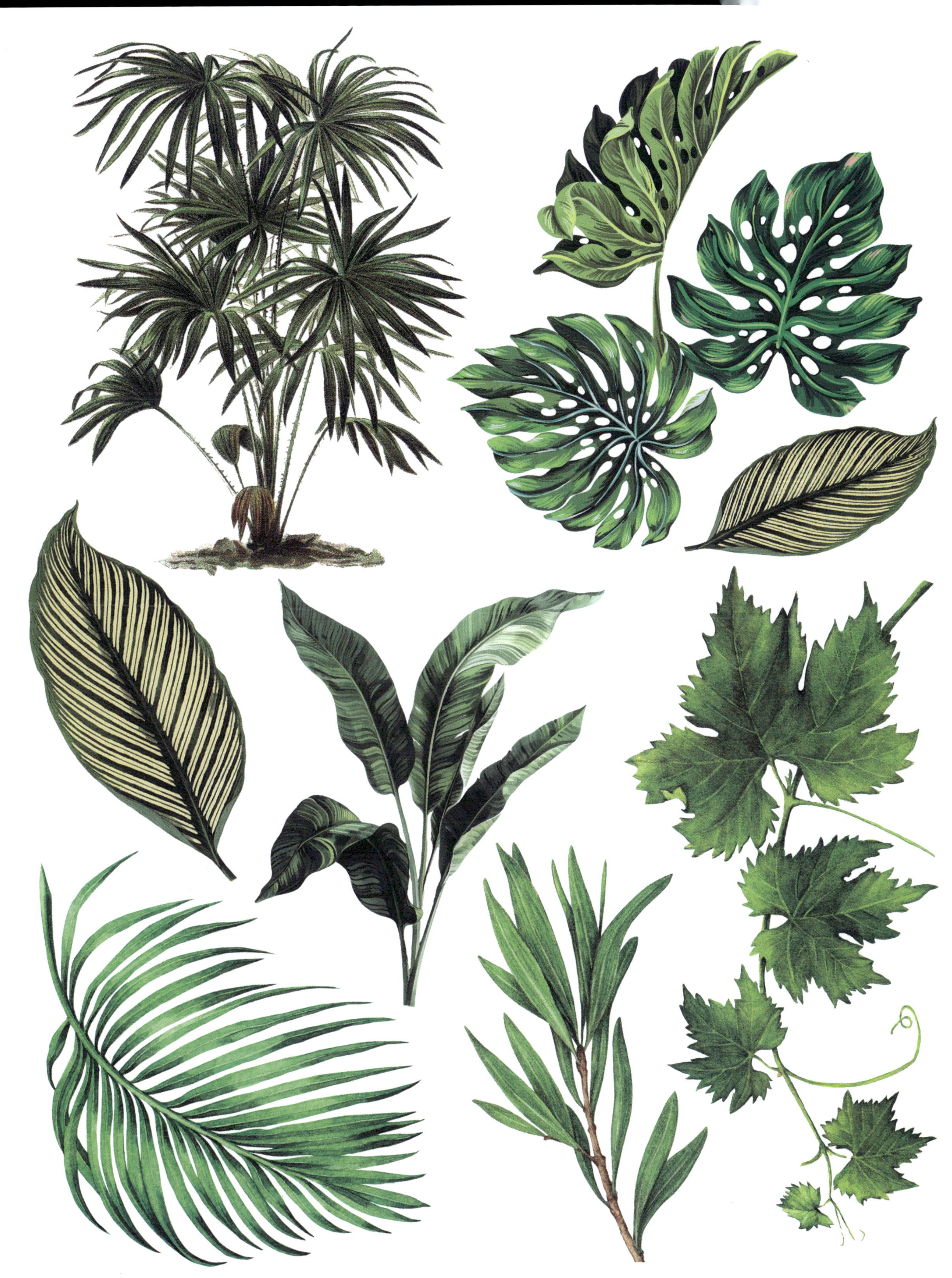

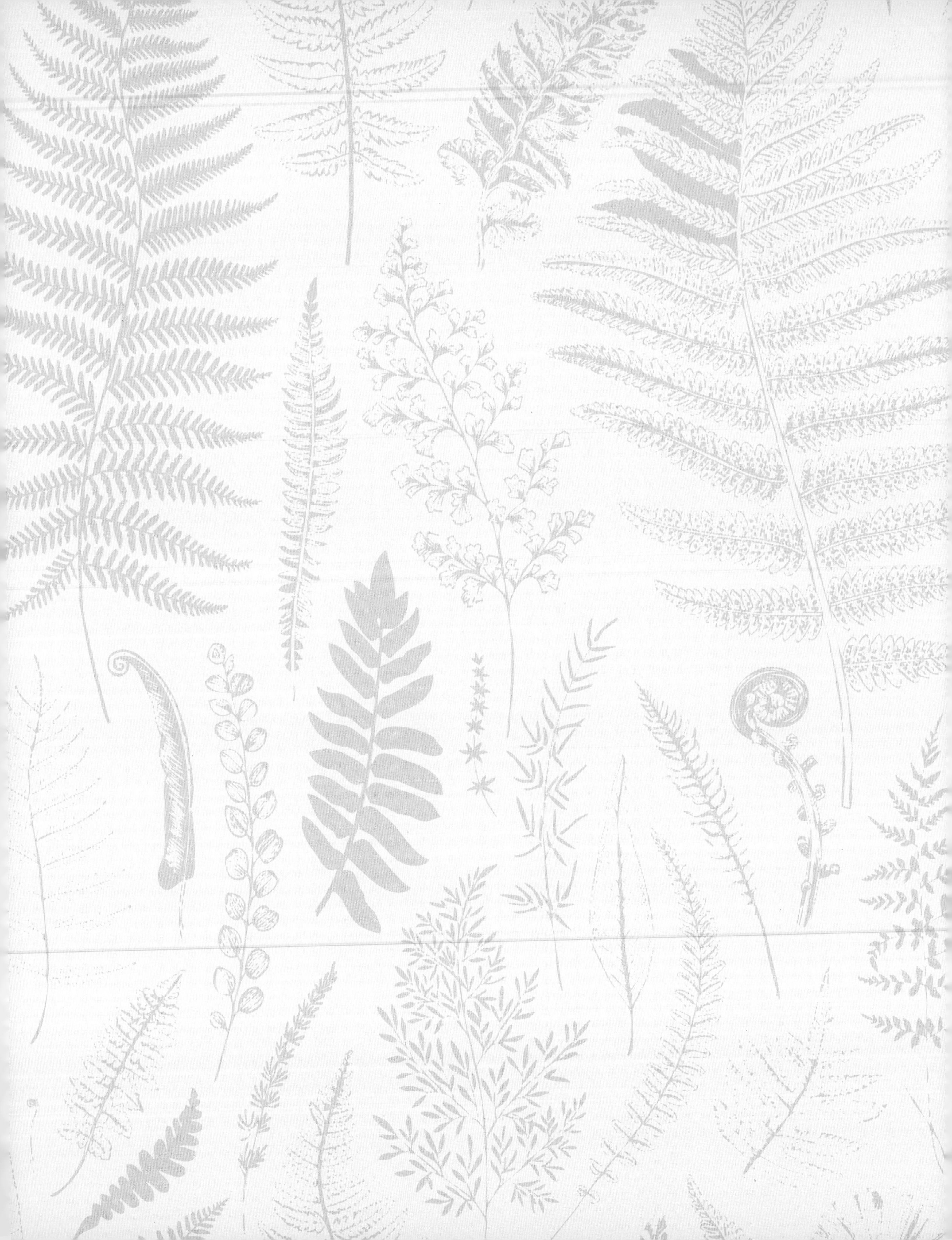

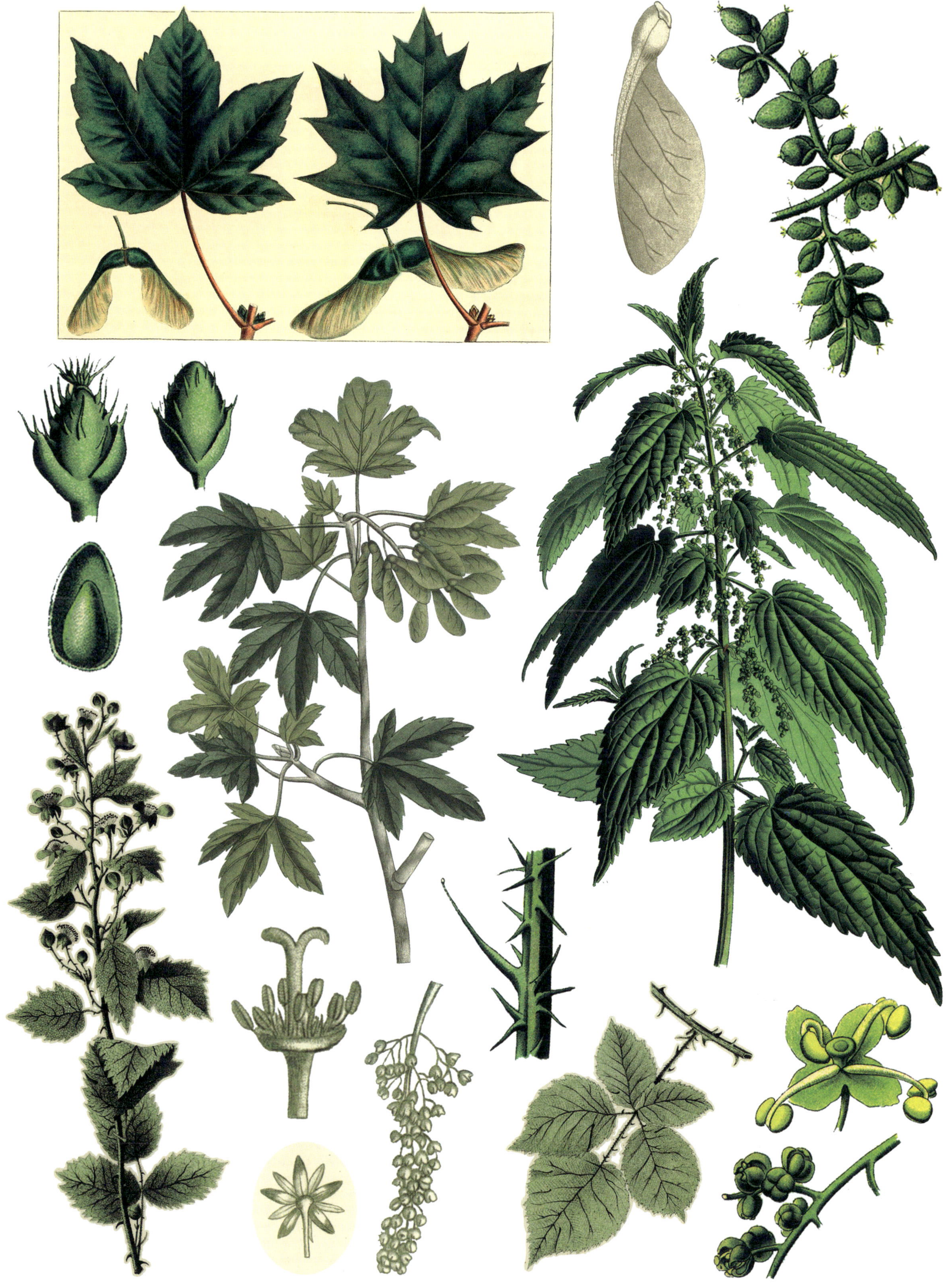

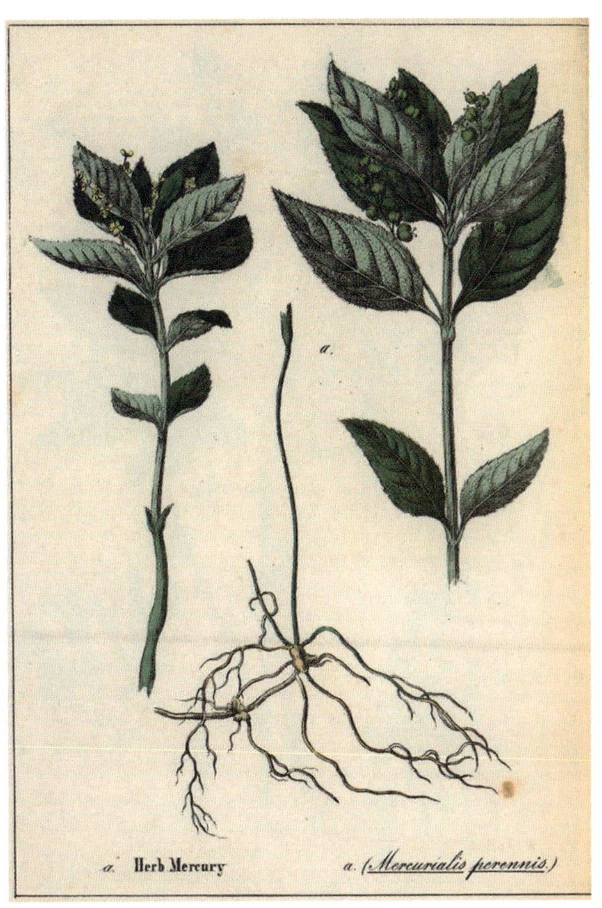
a. Herb Mercury
a. (Mercurialis perennis.)

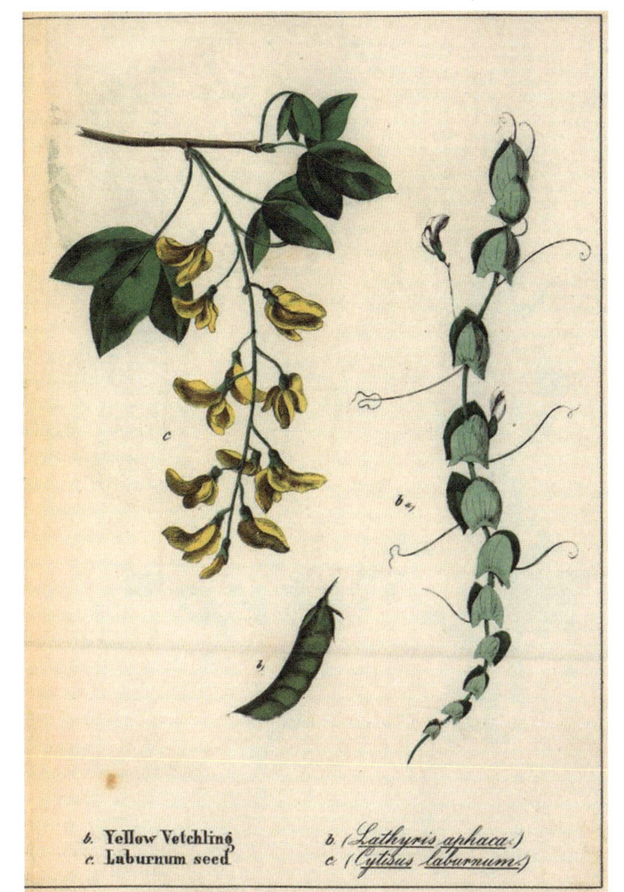
b. Yellow Vetchling
c. Laburnum seed
b (Lathyris aphaca.)
c (Cytisus laburnum)

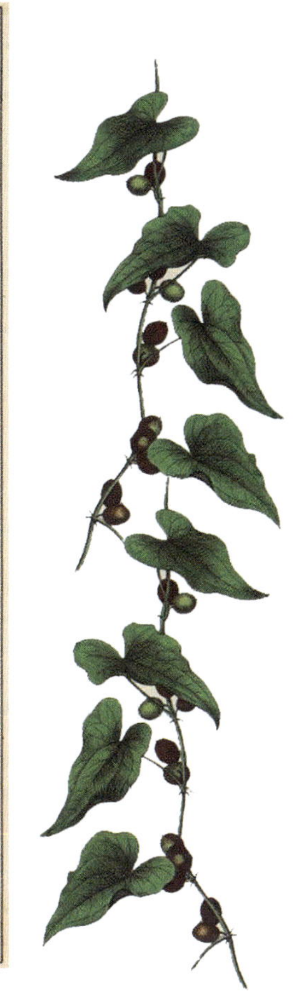

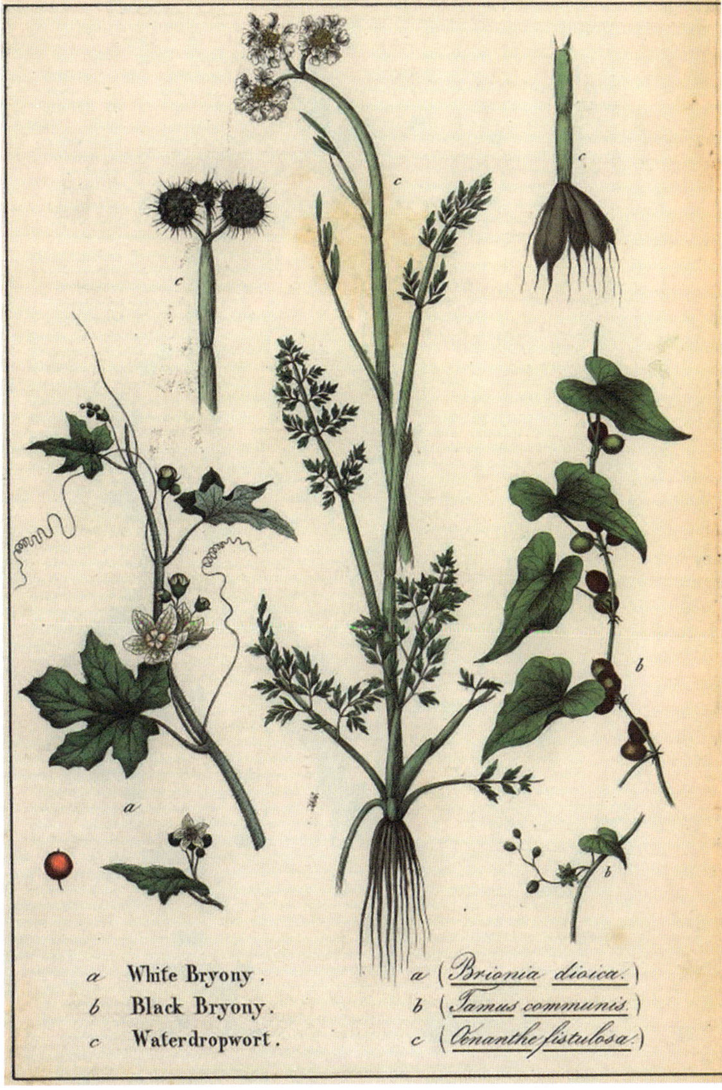
a White Bryony.
b Black Bryony.
c Waterdropwort.
a (Brionia dioica.)
b (Tamus communis.)
c (Oenanthe fistulosa.)

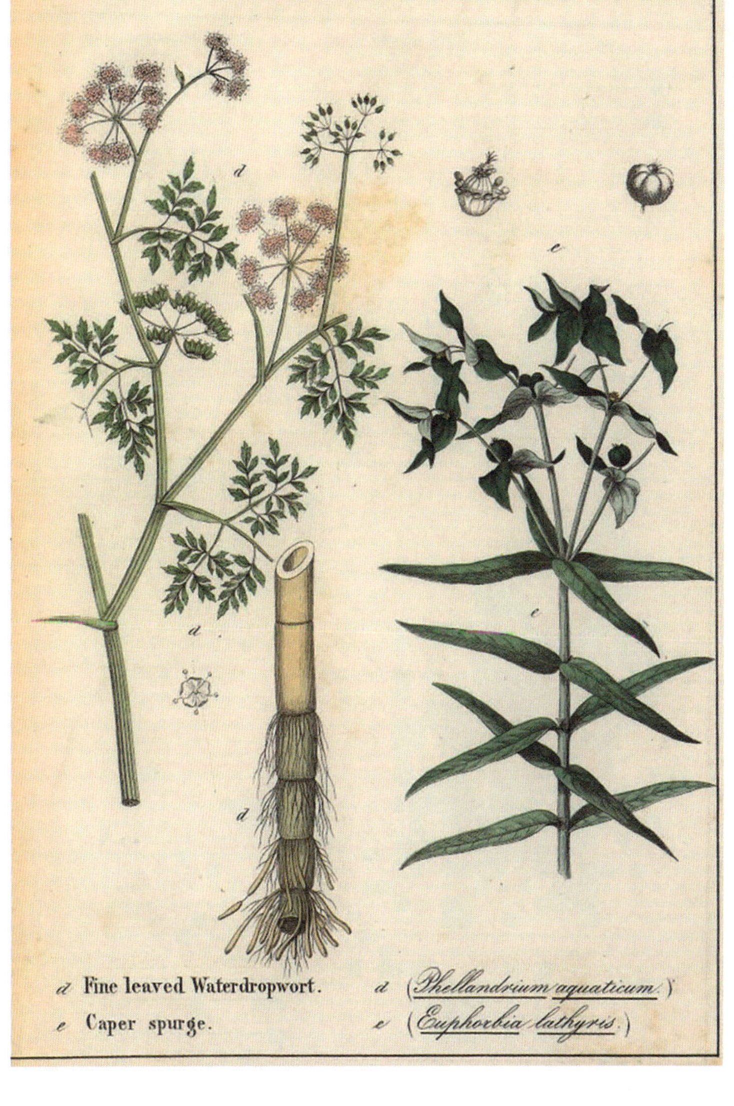
d Fine leaved Waterdropwort.
e Caper spurge.
d (Phellandrium aquaticum.)
e (Euphorbia lathyris.)

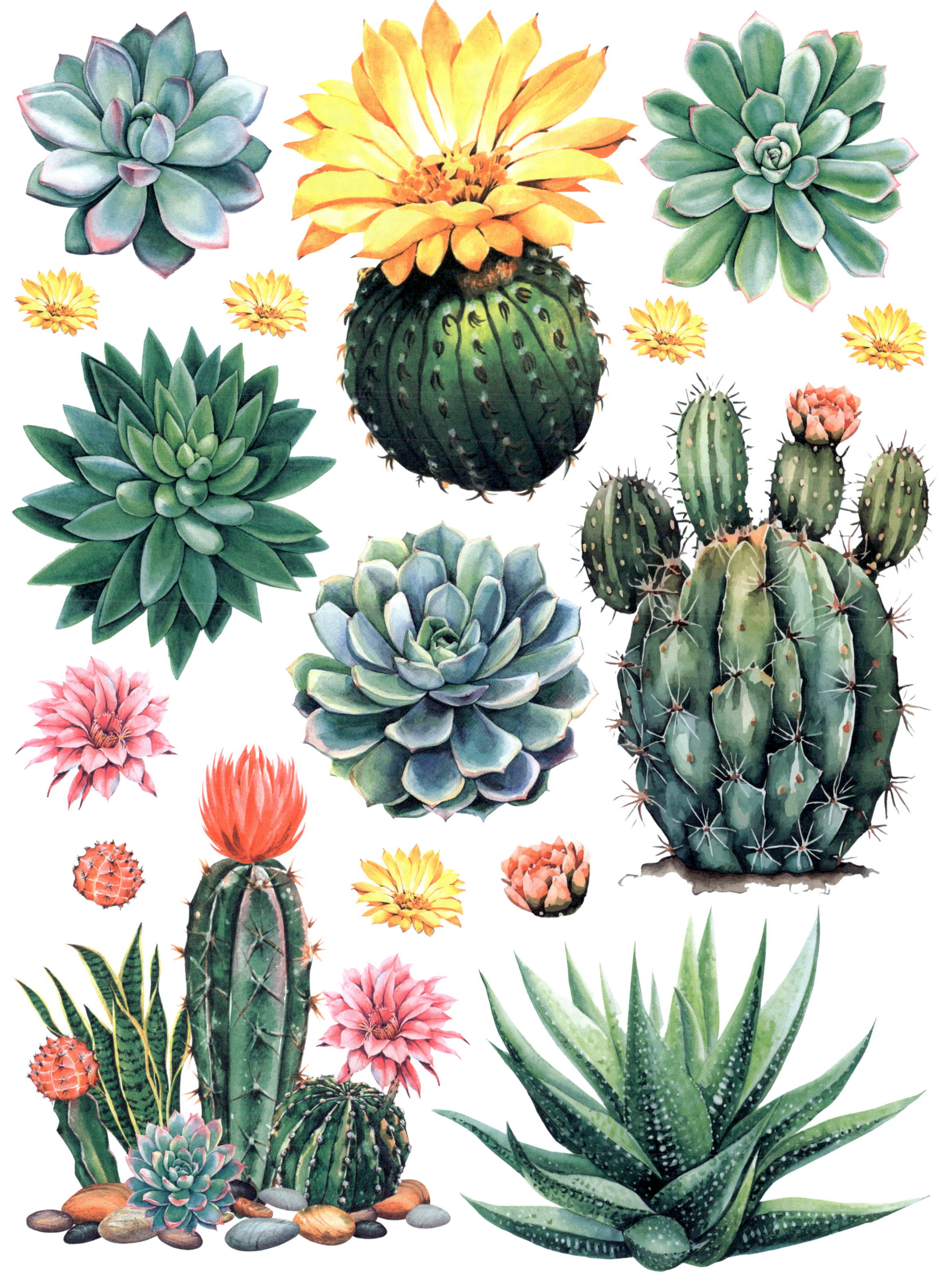

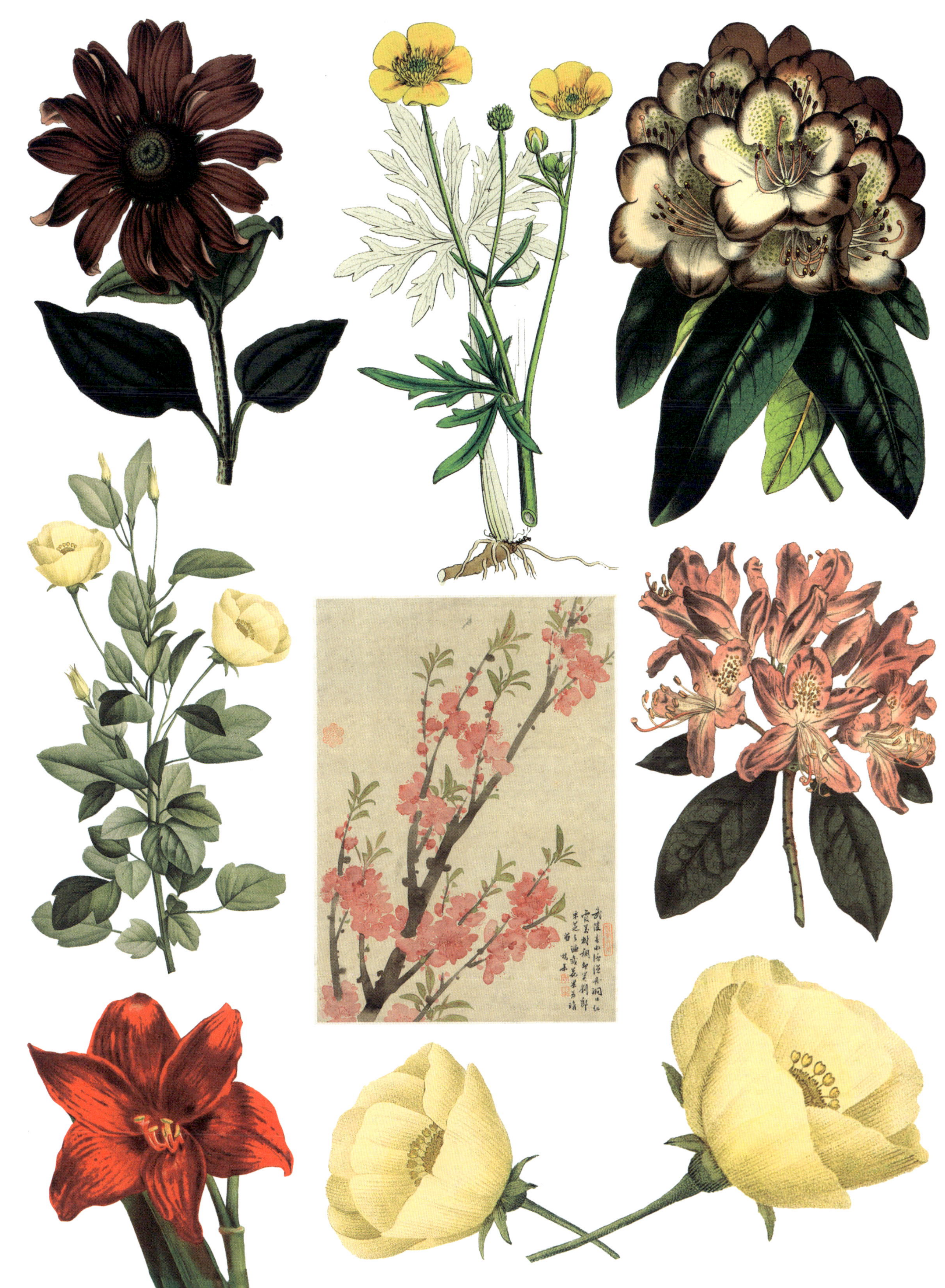

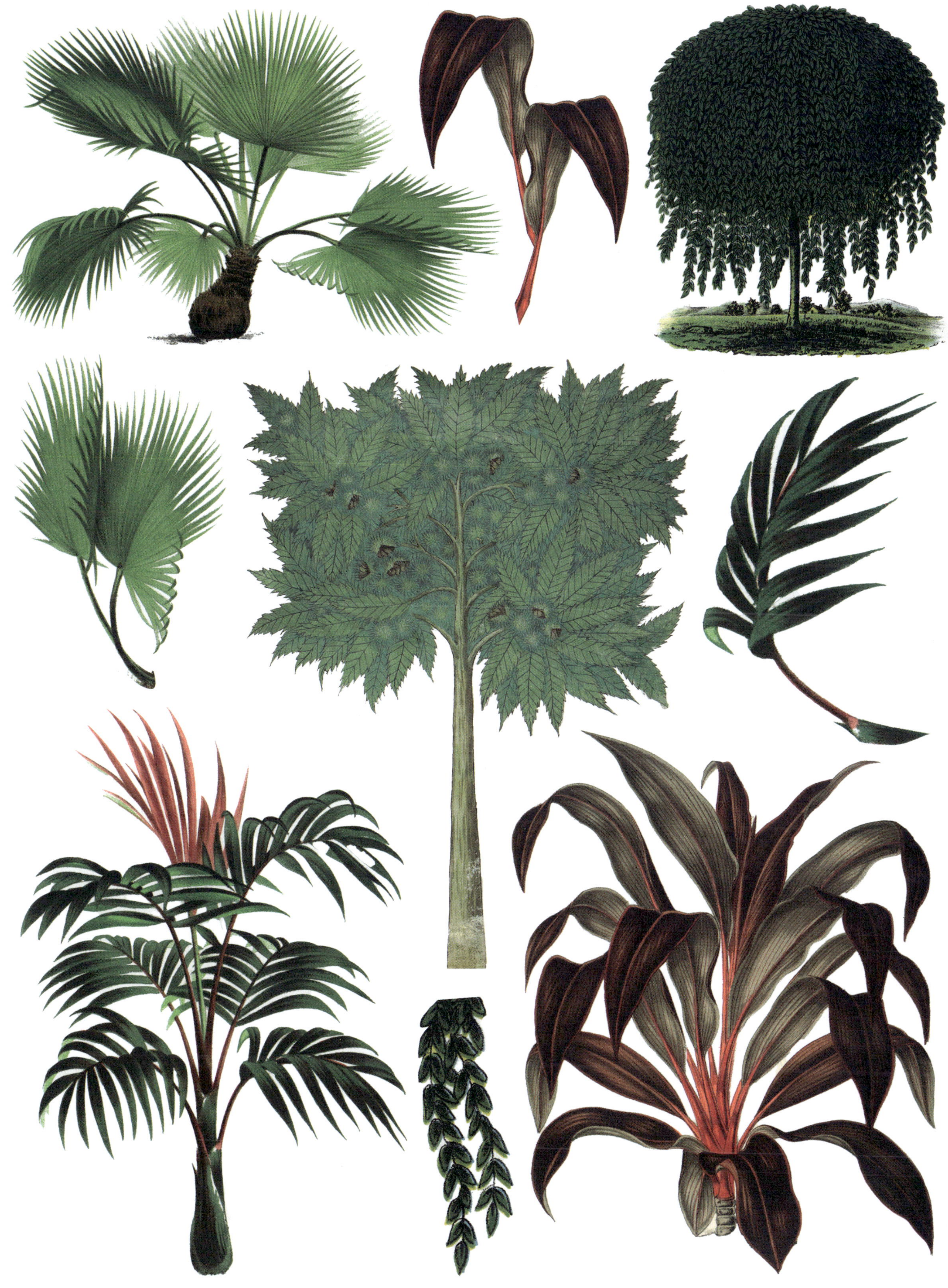

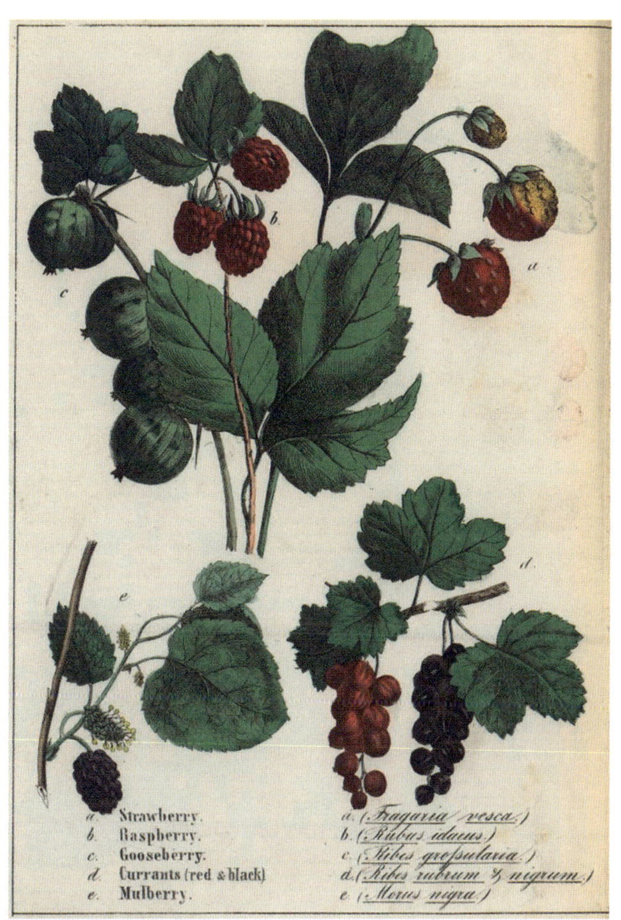
a. Strawberry.
b. Raspberry.
c. Gooseberry.
d. Currants (red & black)
e. Mulberry.
a. (Fragaria vesca.)
b. (Rubus idaeus.)
c. (Ribes grossularia.)
d. (Ribes rubrum & nigrum.)
e. (Morus nigra.)

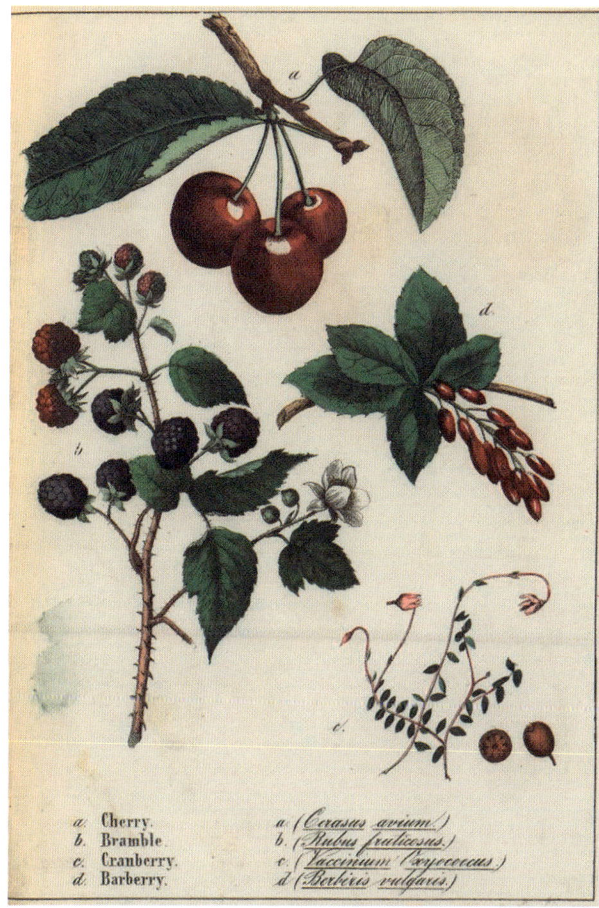
a. Cherry.
b. Bramble.
c. Cranberry.
d. Barberry.
a. (Cerasus avium.)
b. (Rubus fruticosus.)
c. (Vaccinium Oxycoccus.)
d. (Berberis vulgaris.)

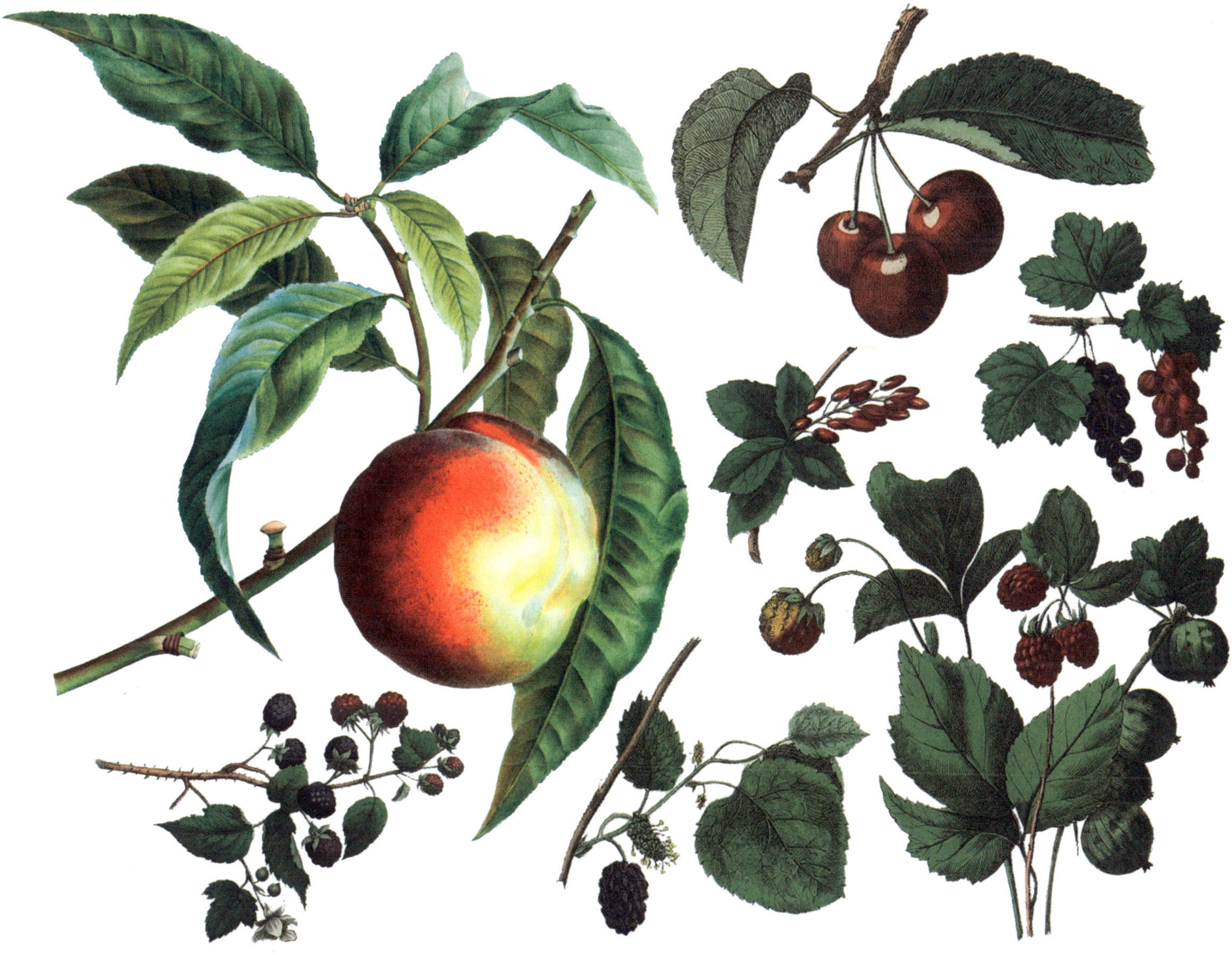

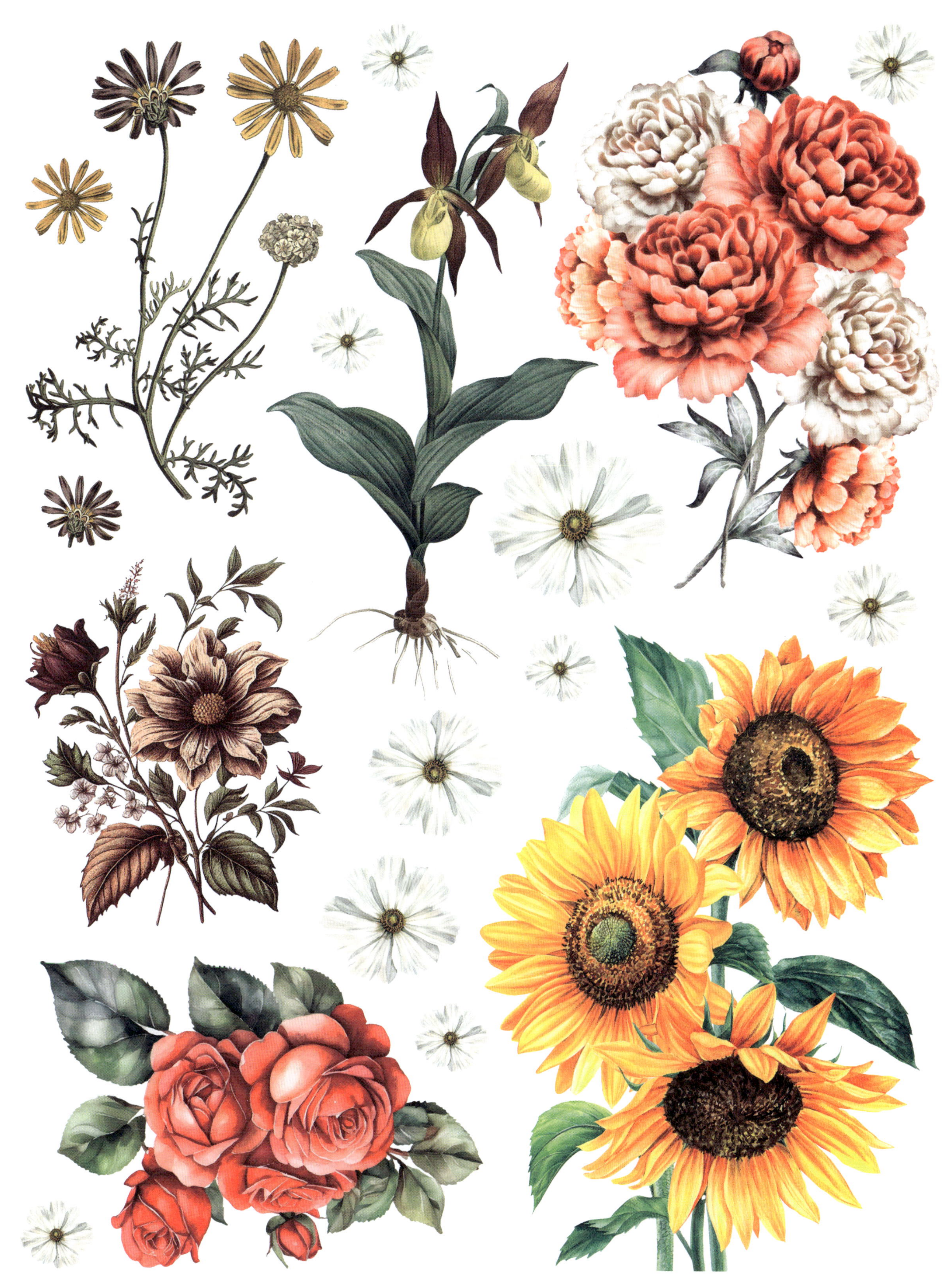

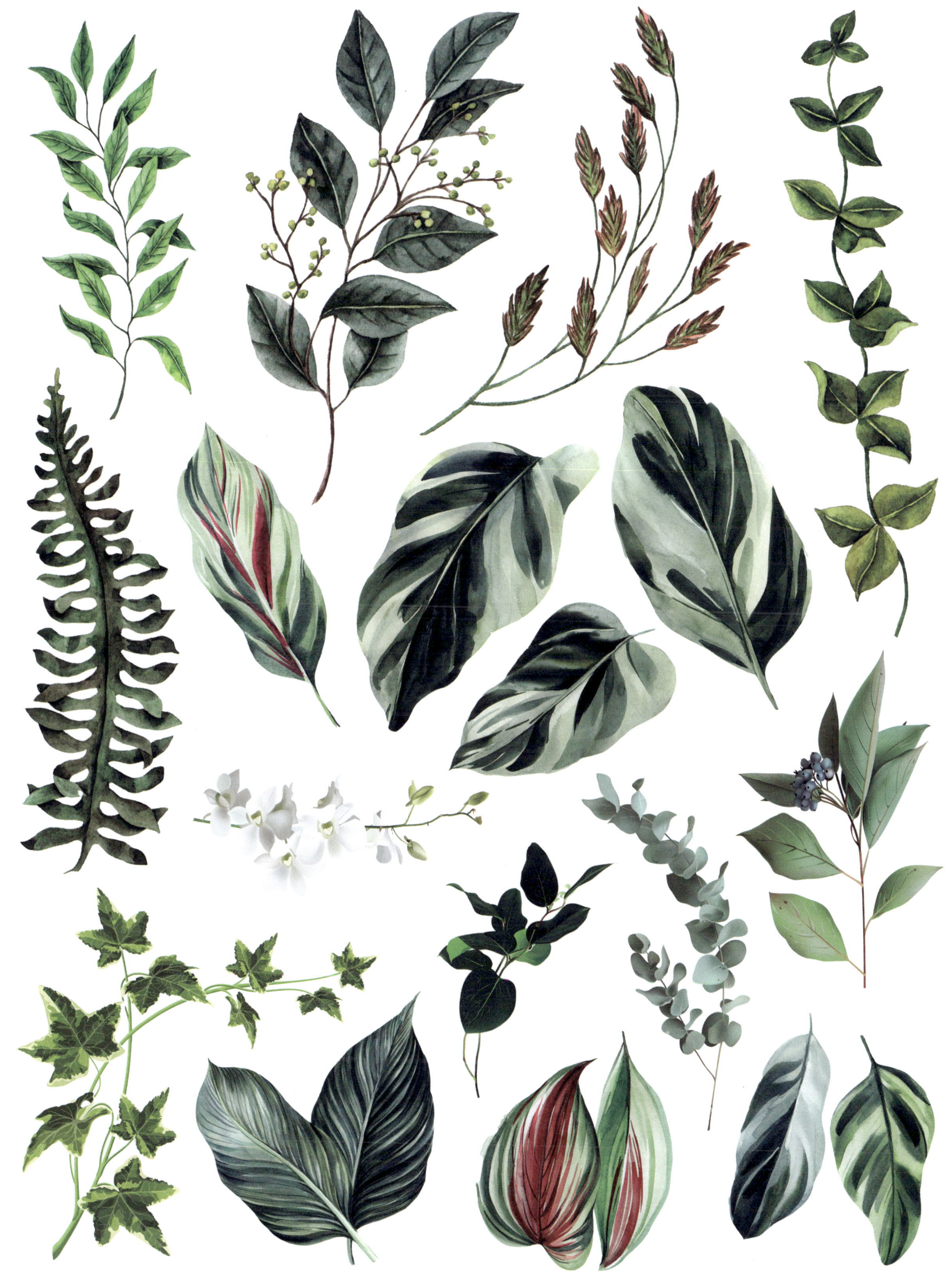

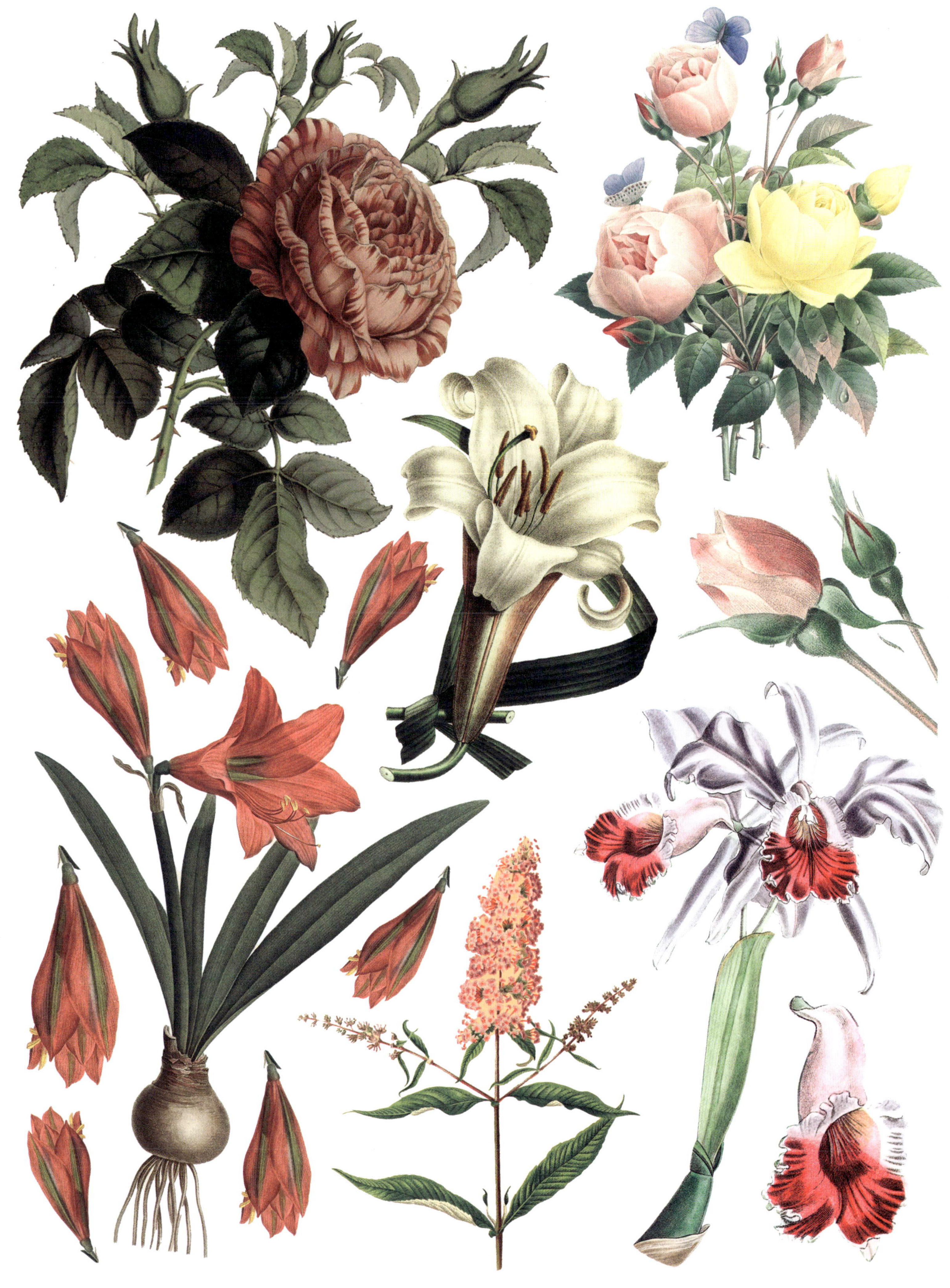

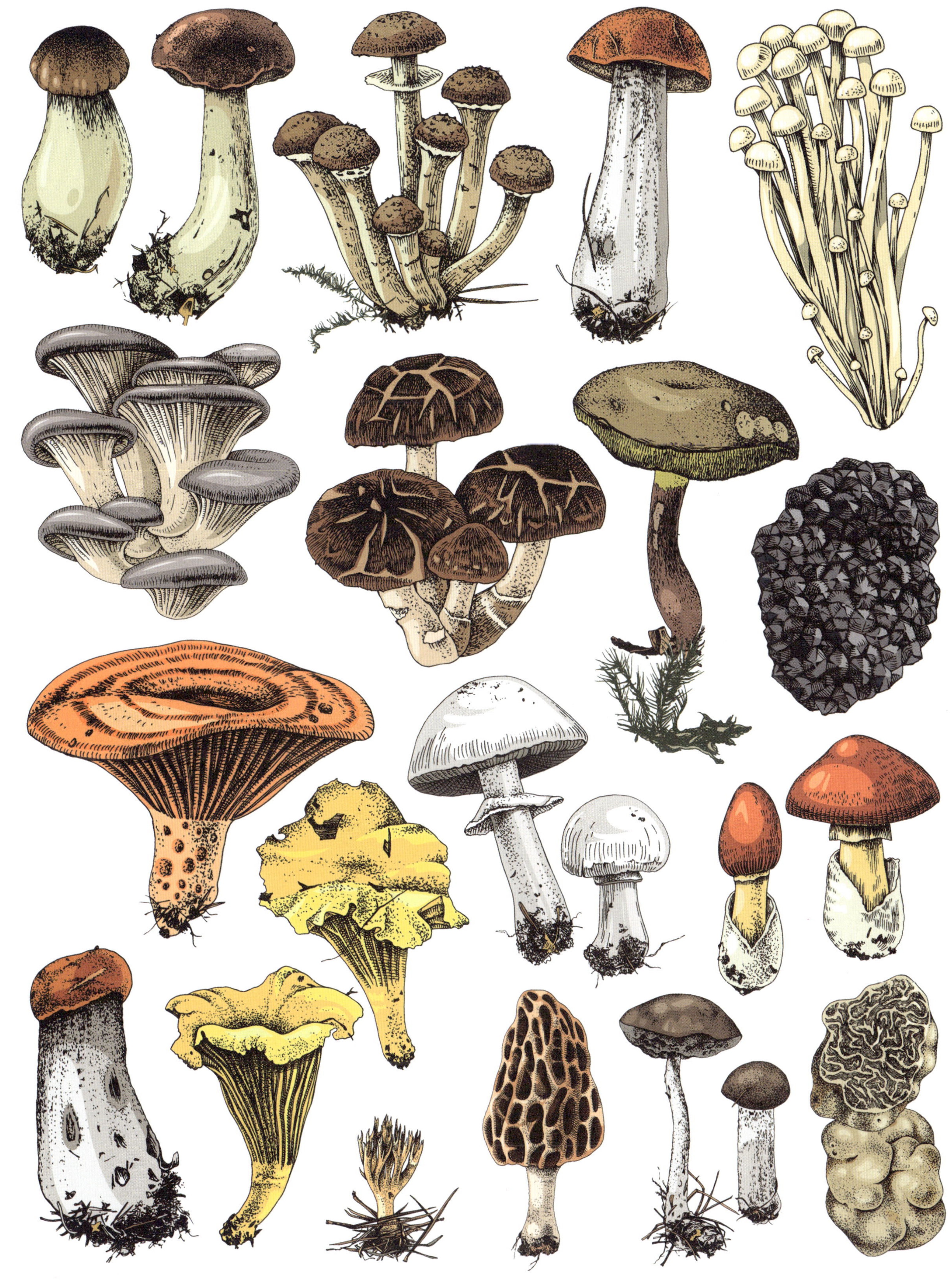

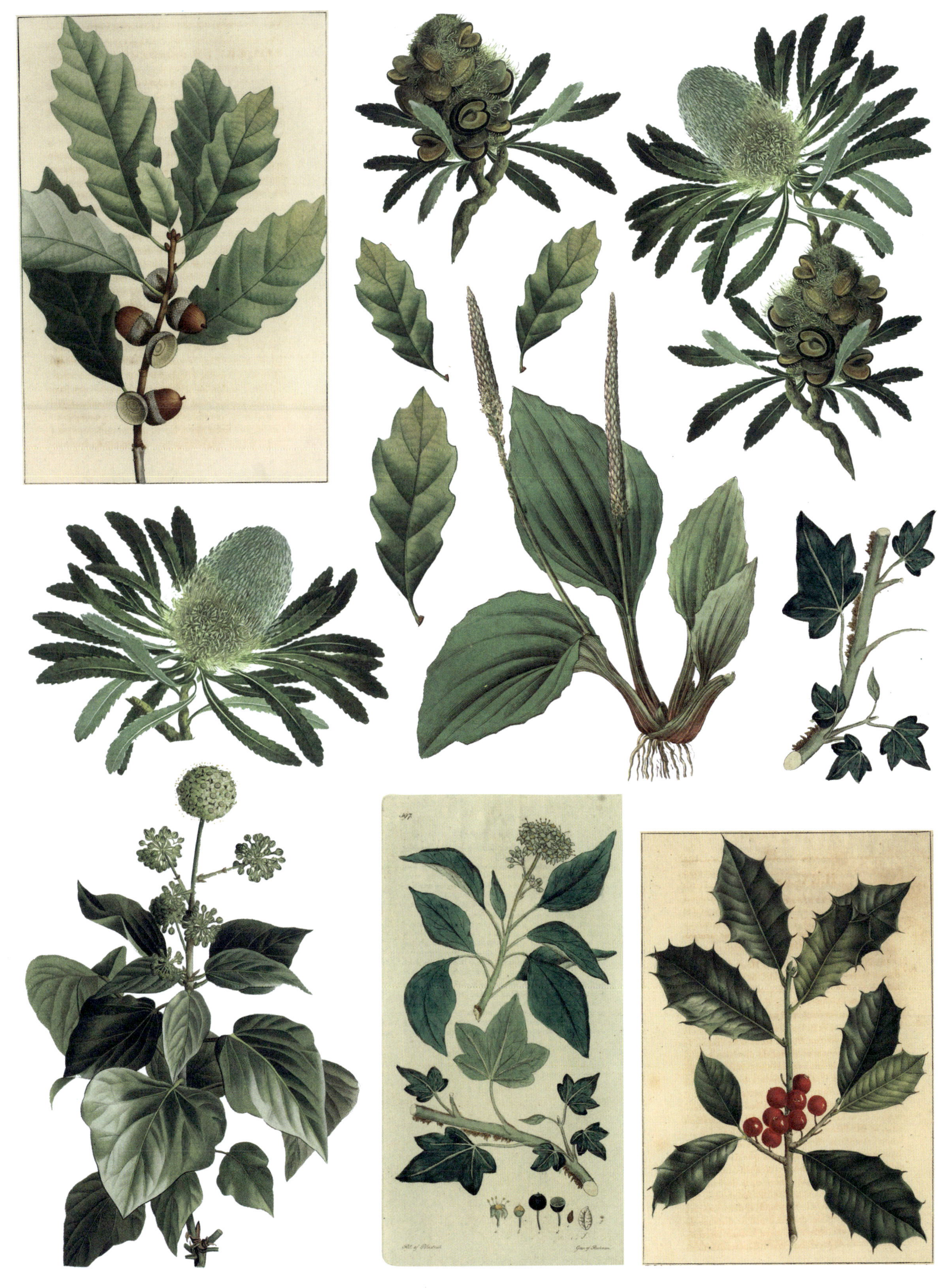
397.

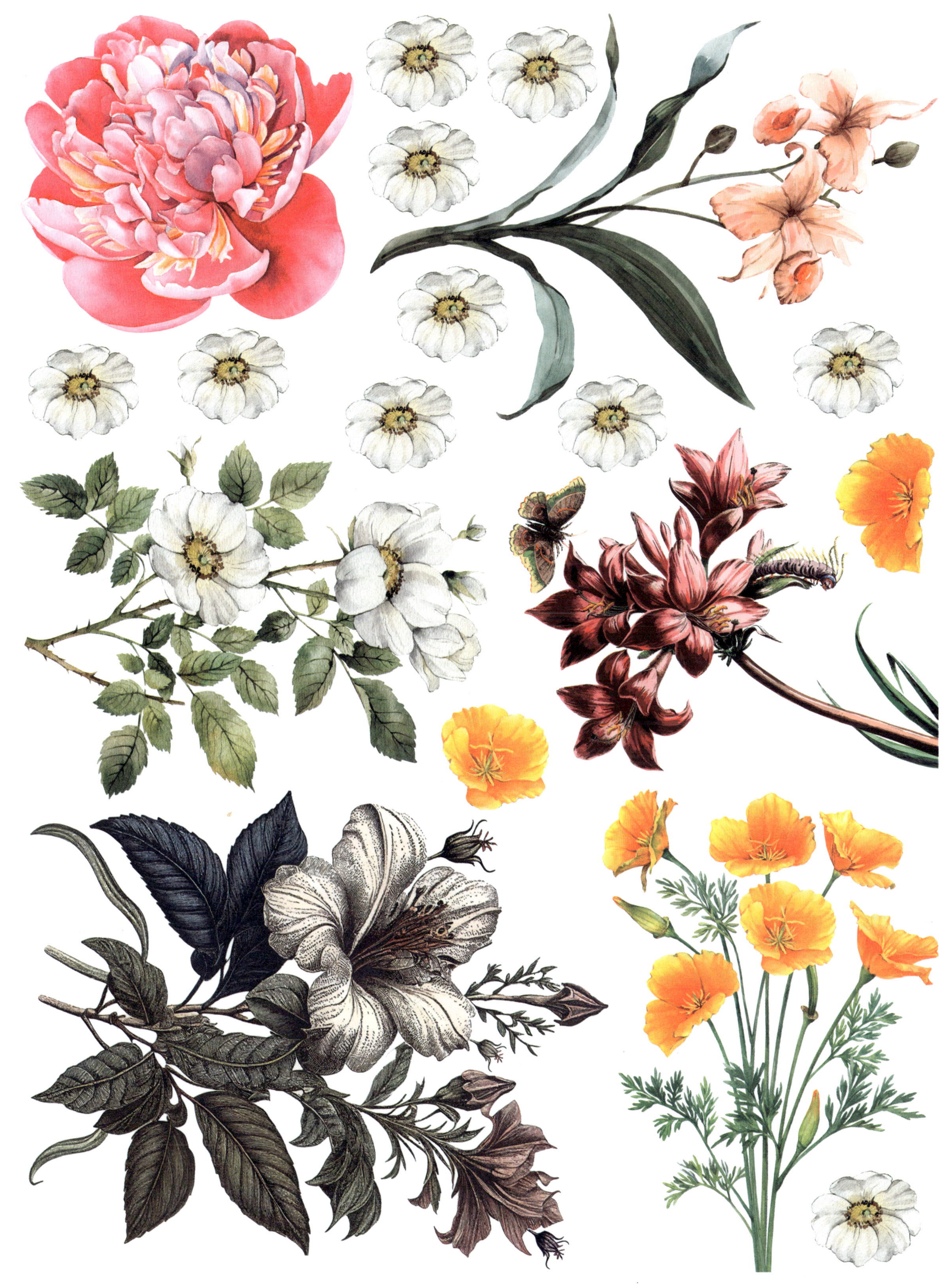

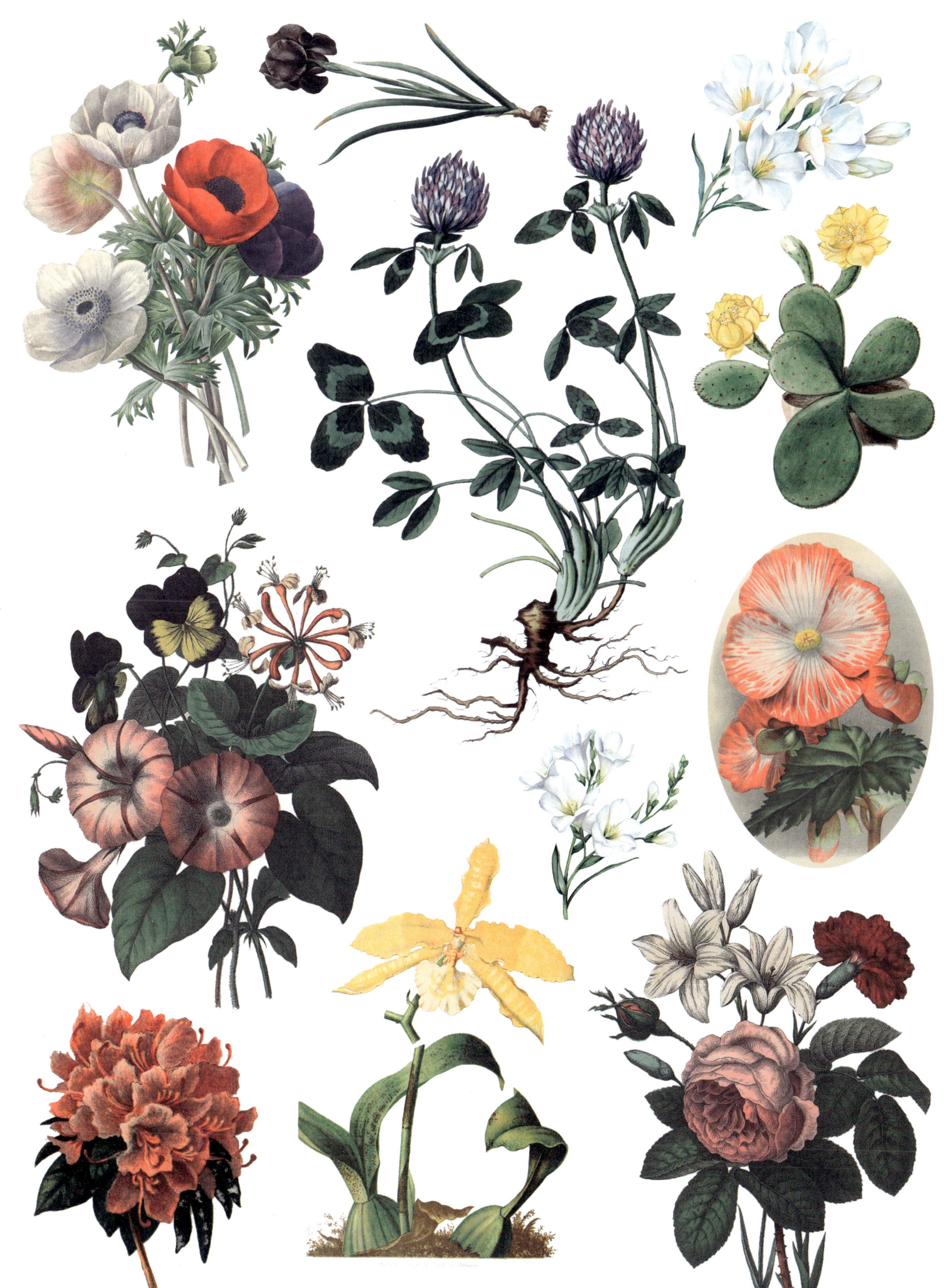

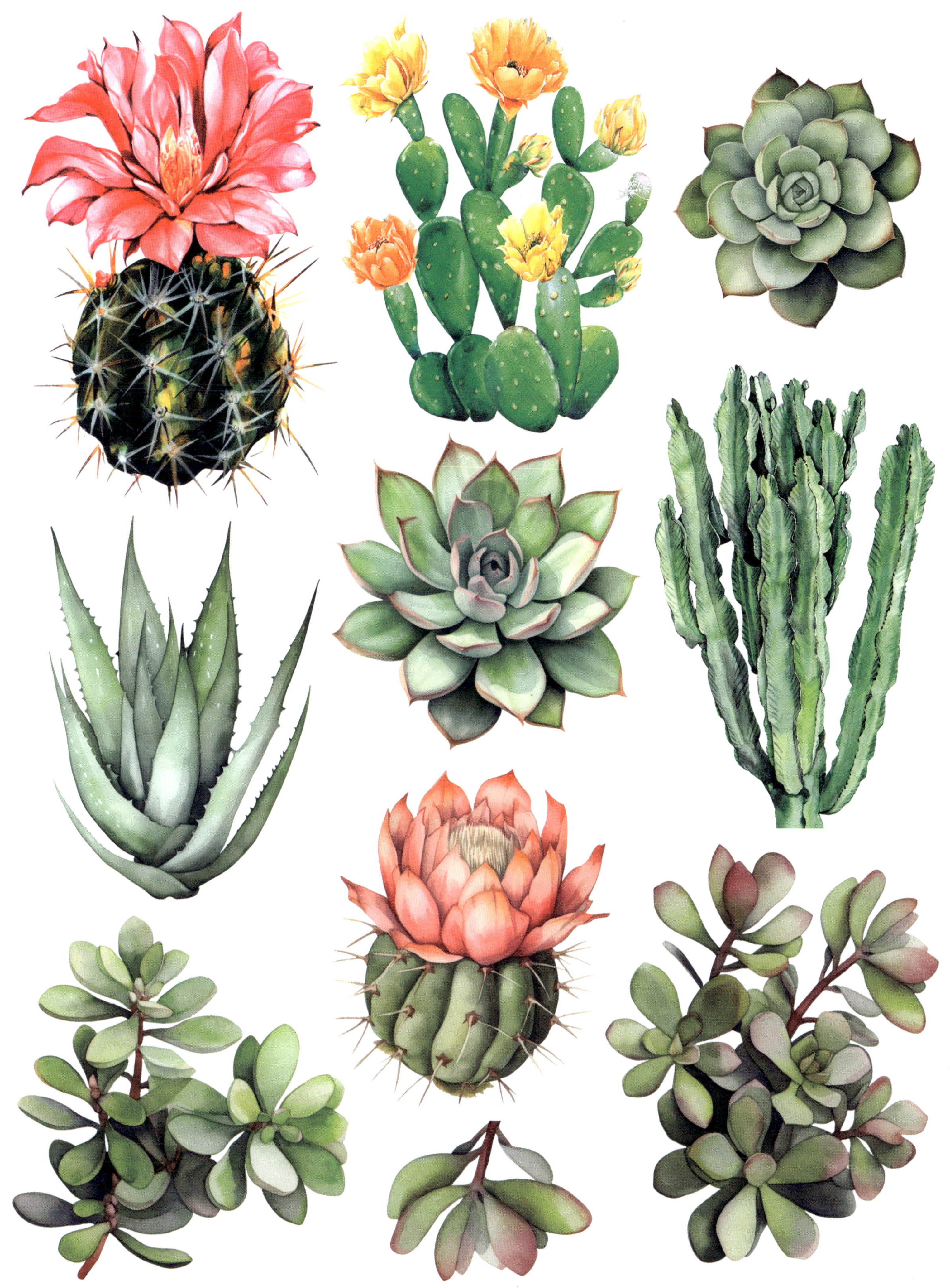

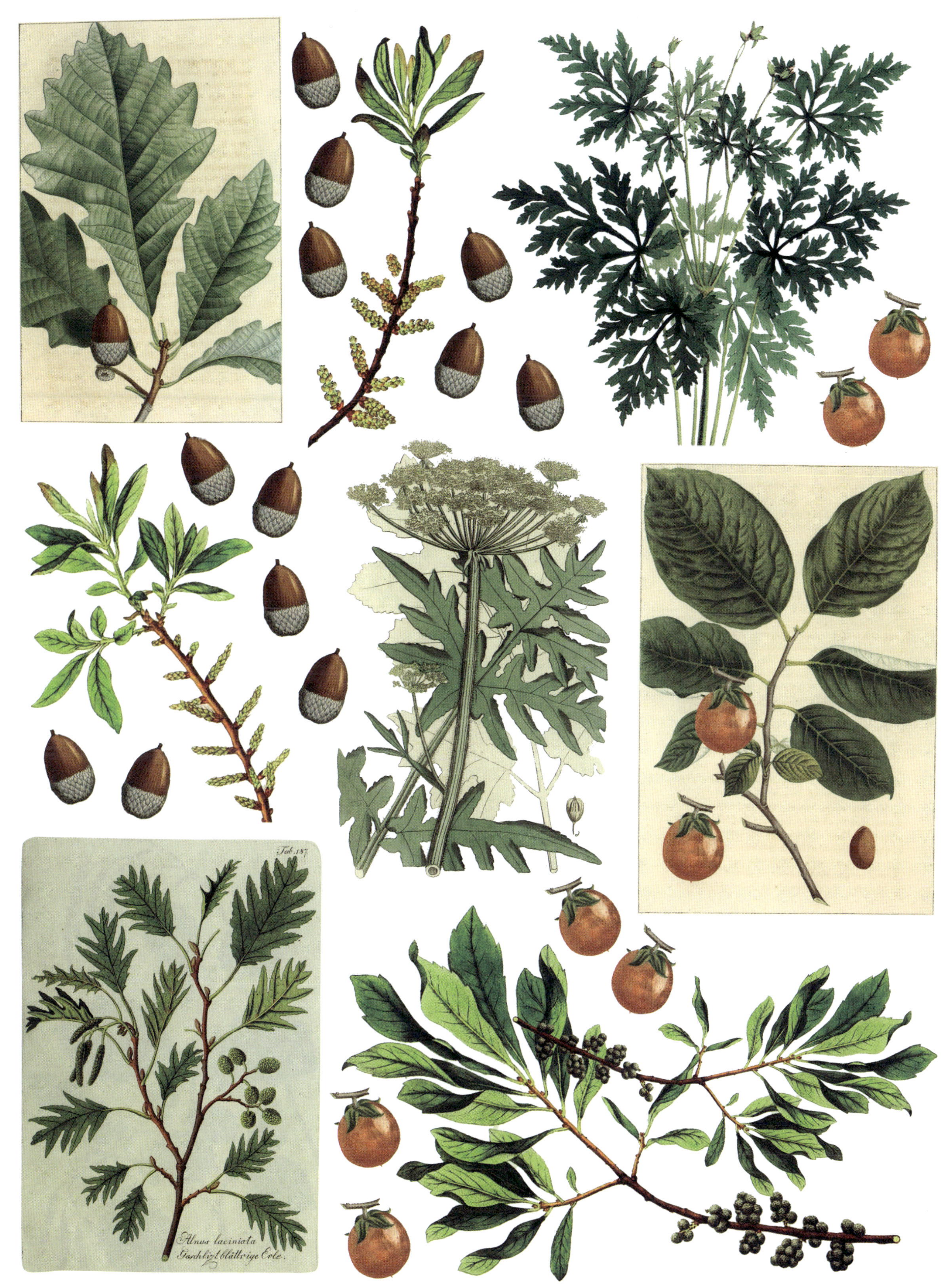
Tab. 187
Alnus laciniata
Garchlizt blättrige Erle.

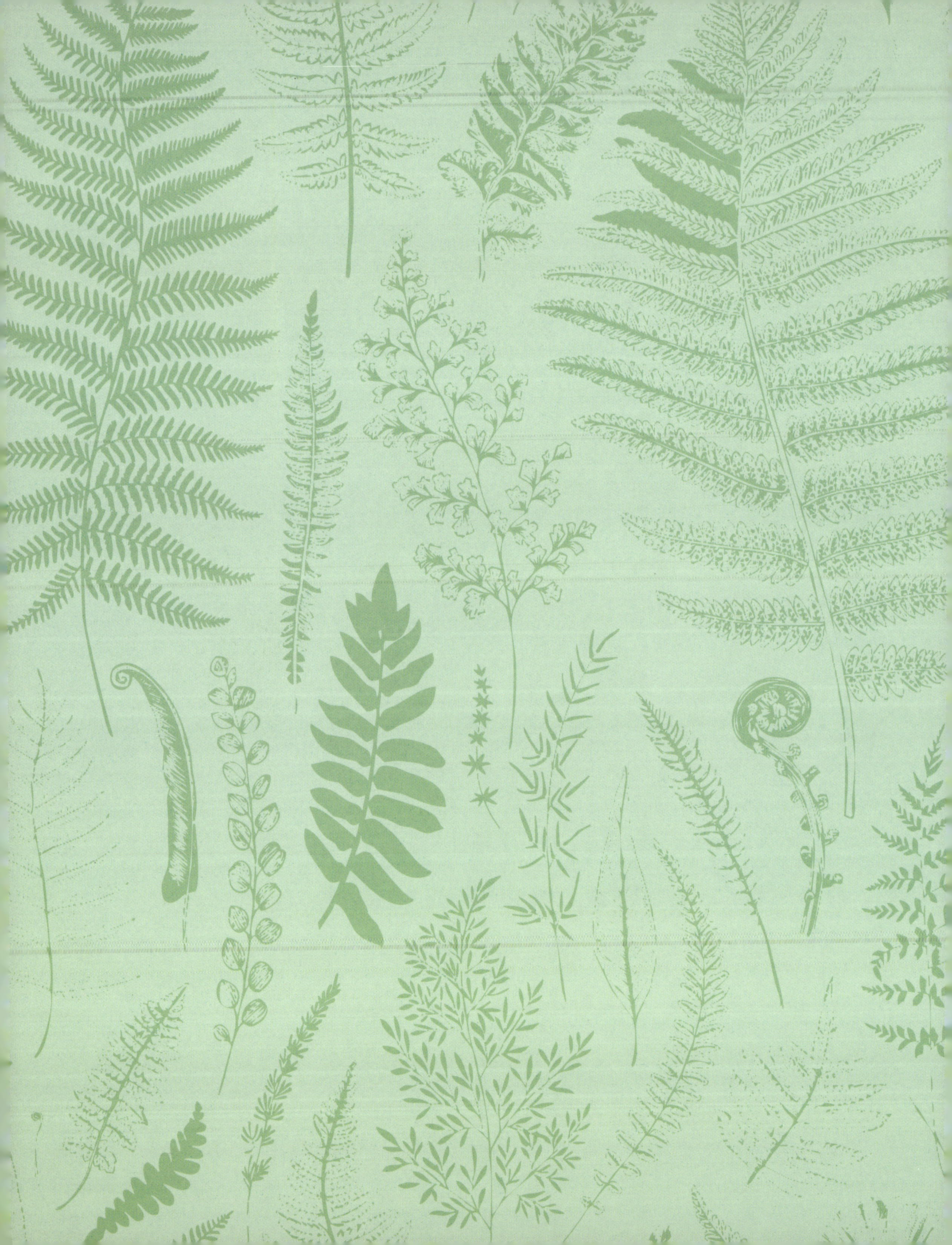

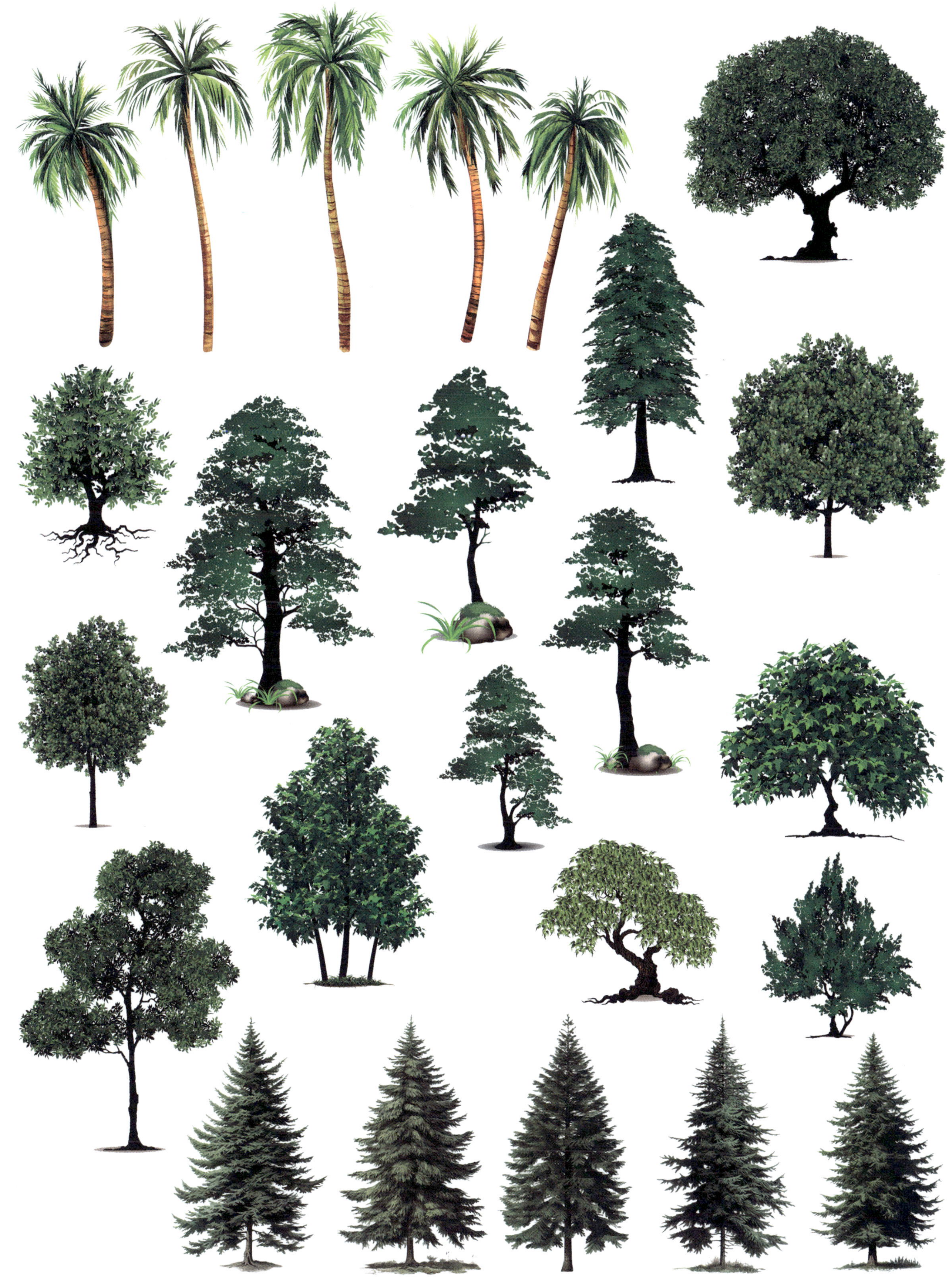

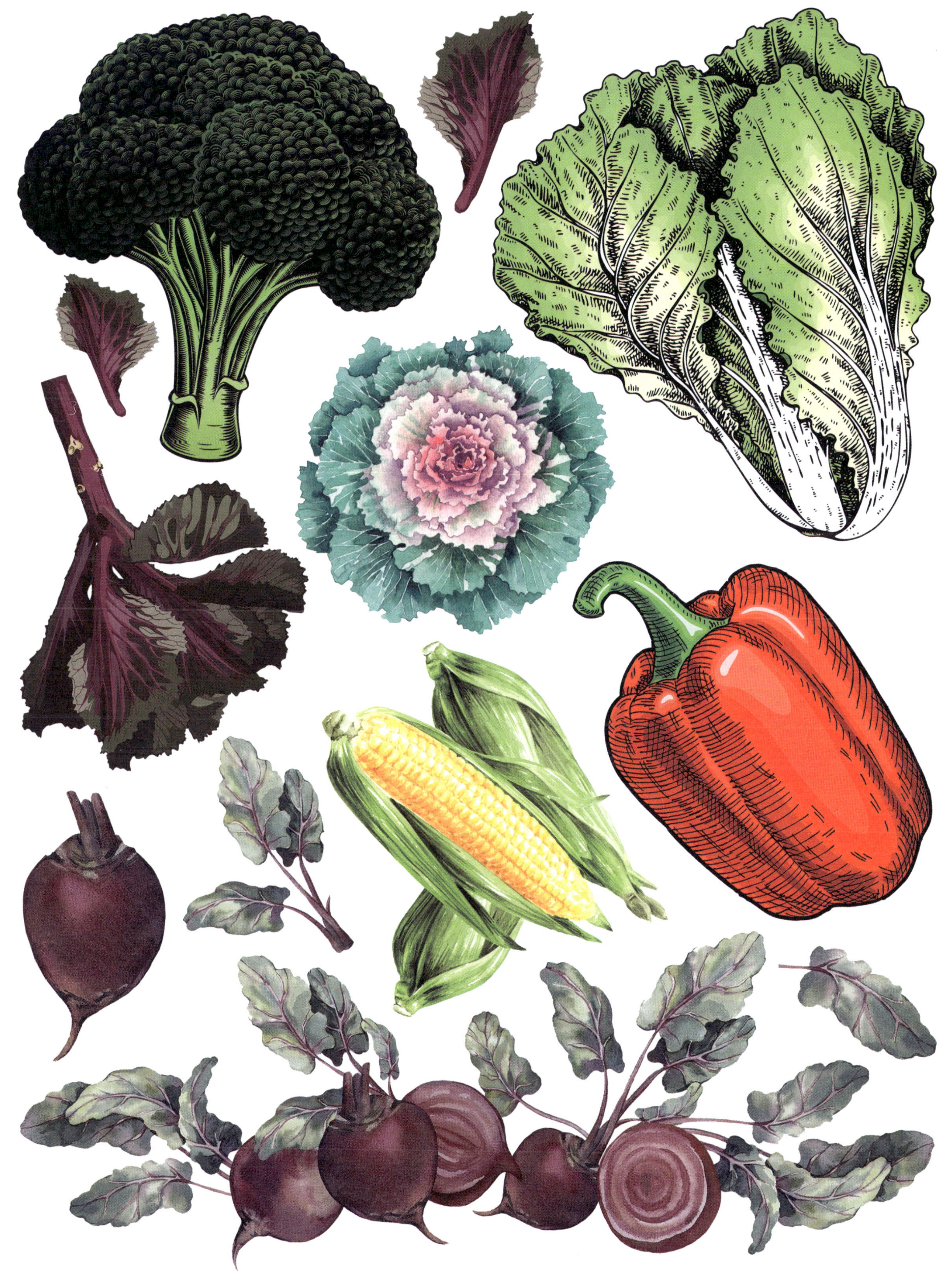

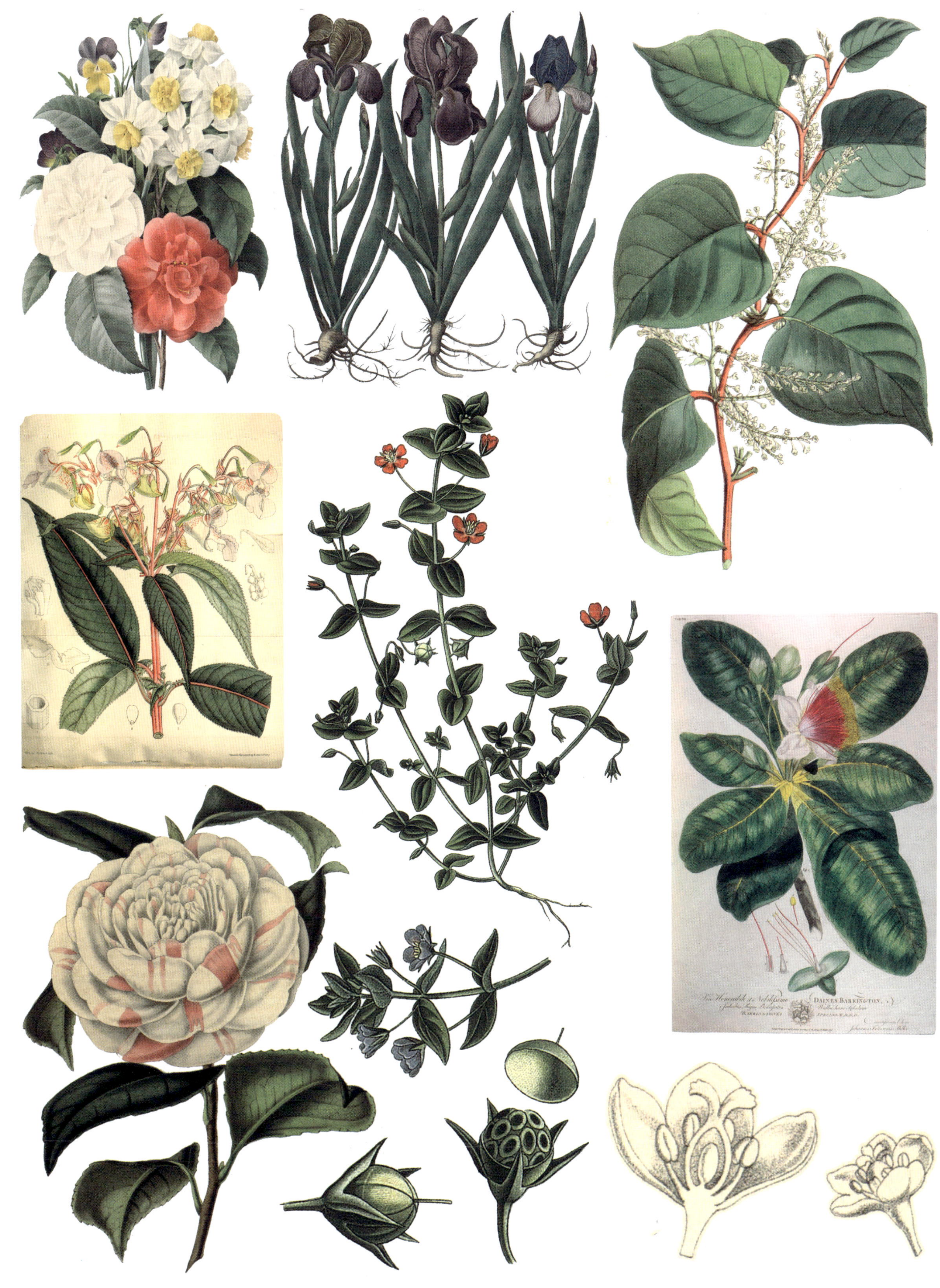
DAINES BARRINGTON,

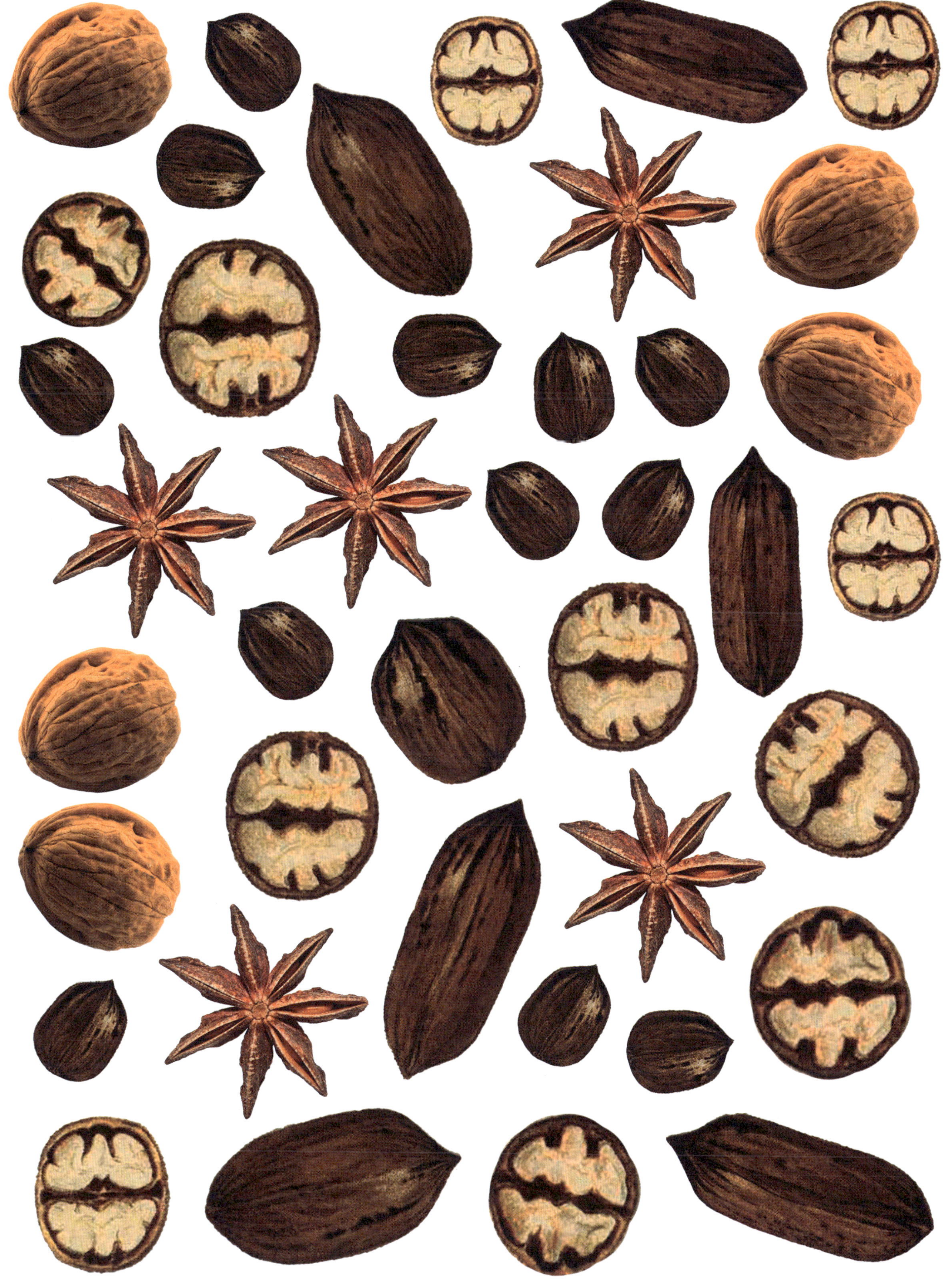

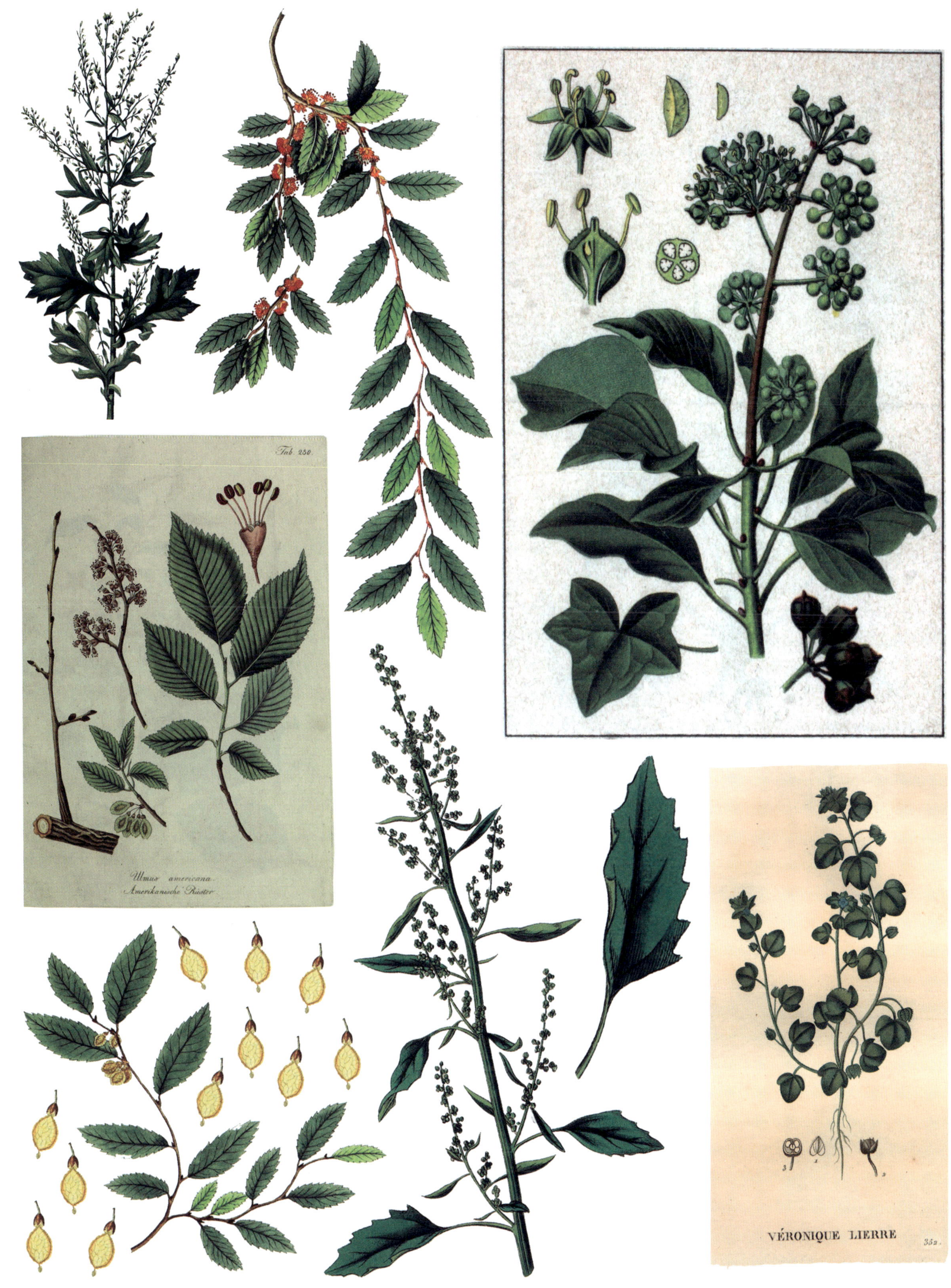
Tab. 250.
Ulmus americana
Amerikanische Rüster
VÉRONIQUE LIERRE
352.

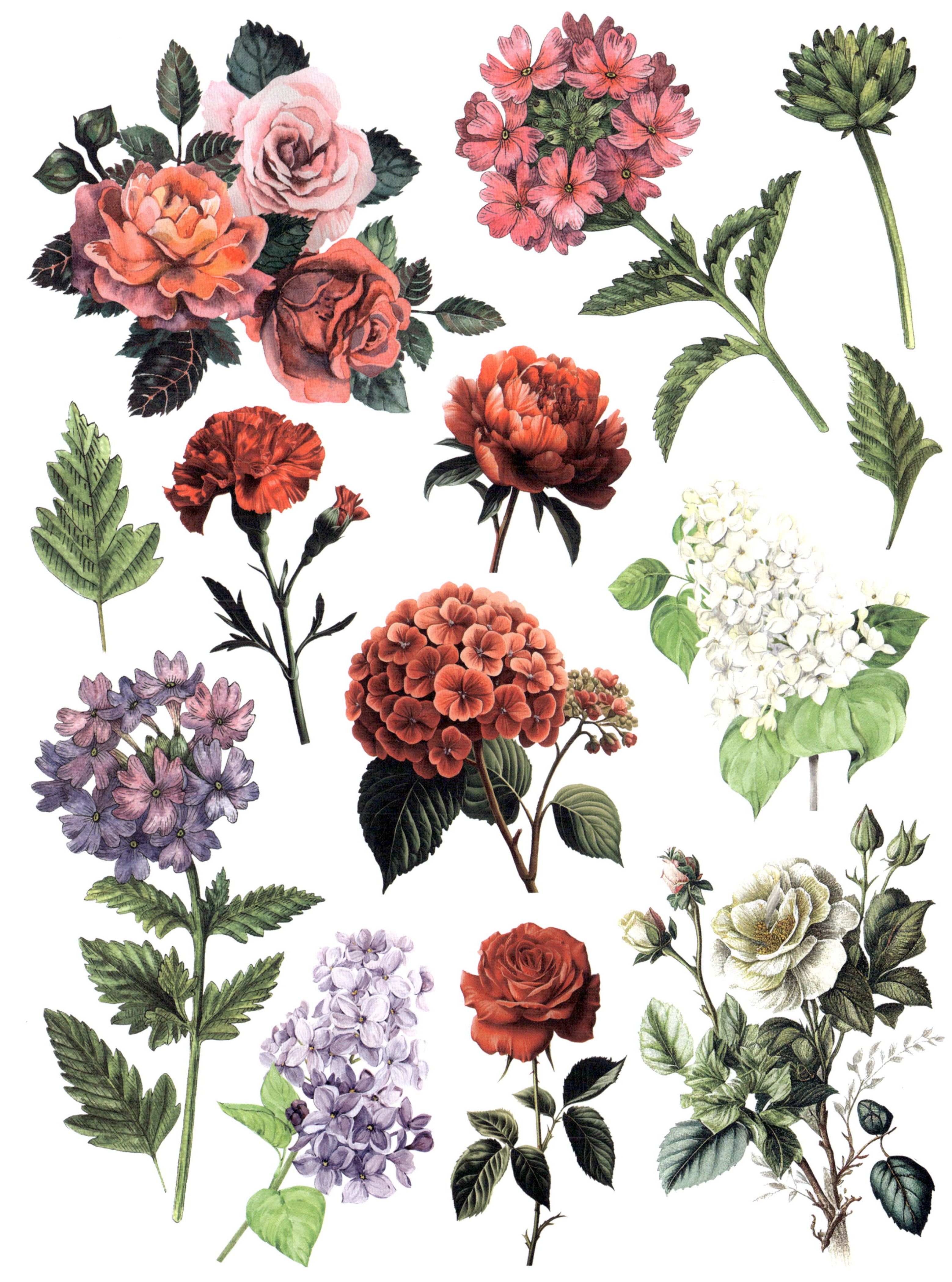

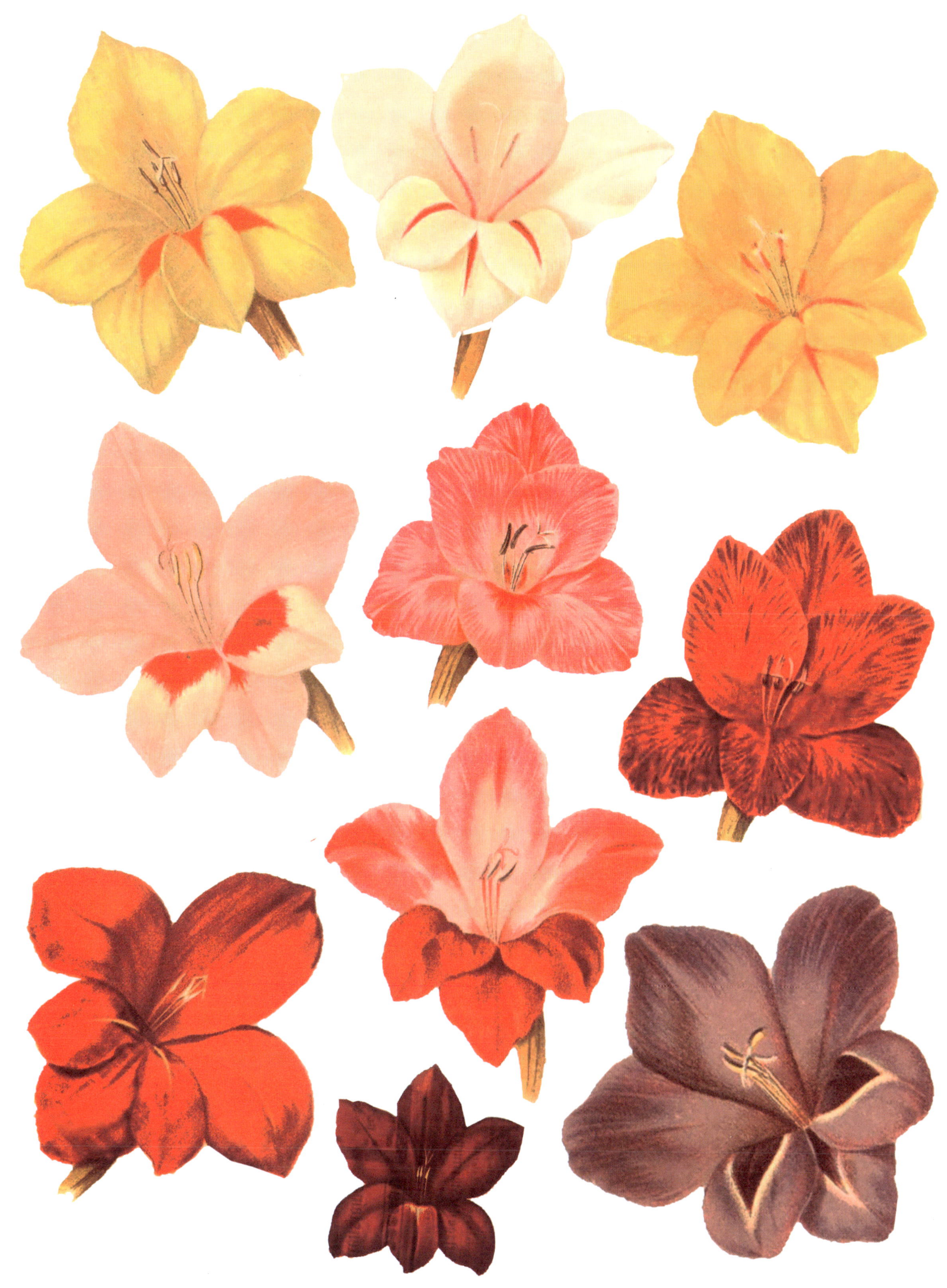

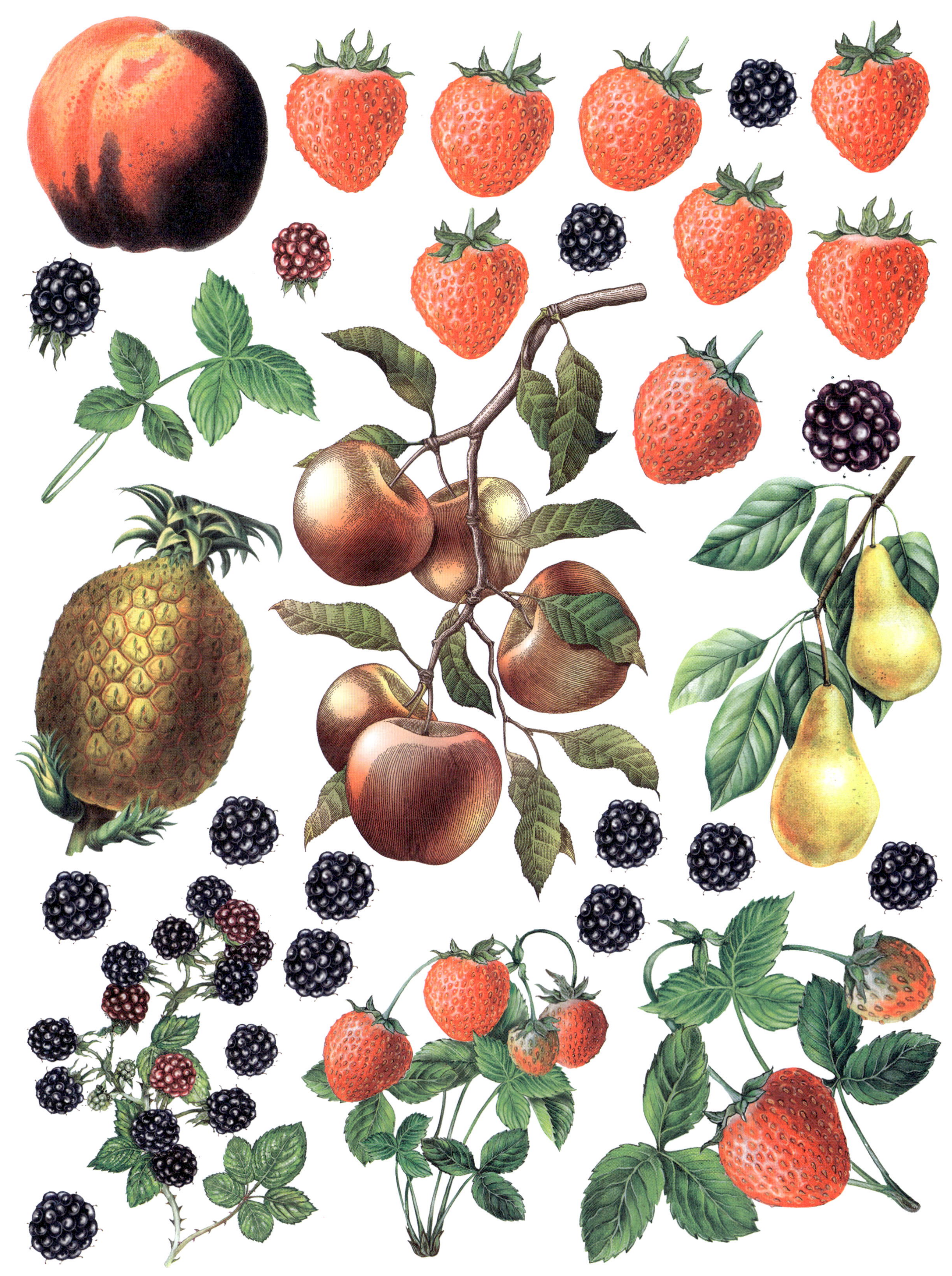

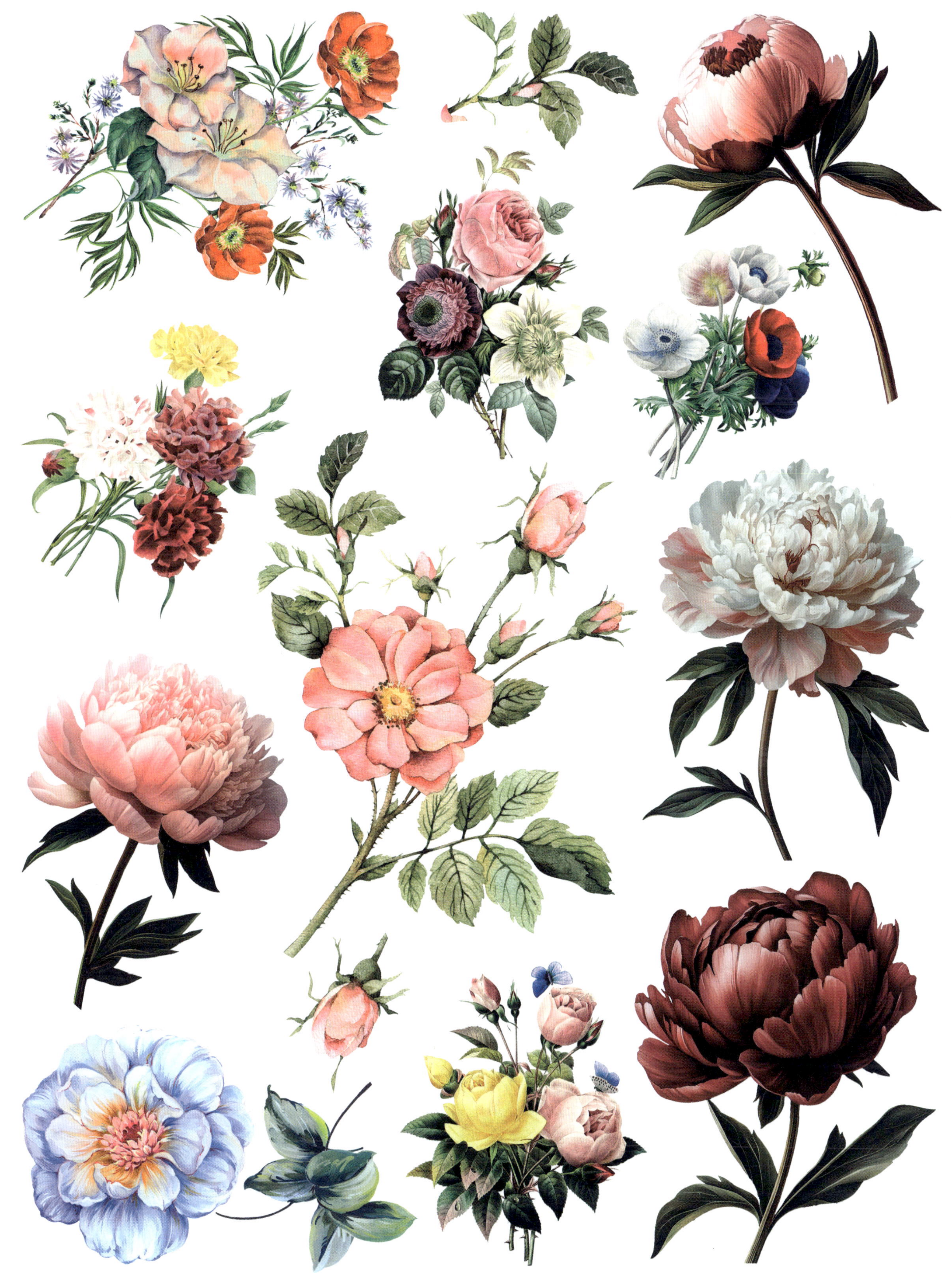

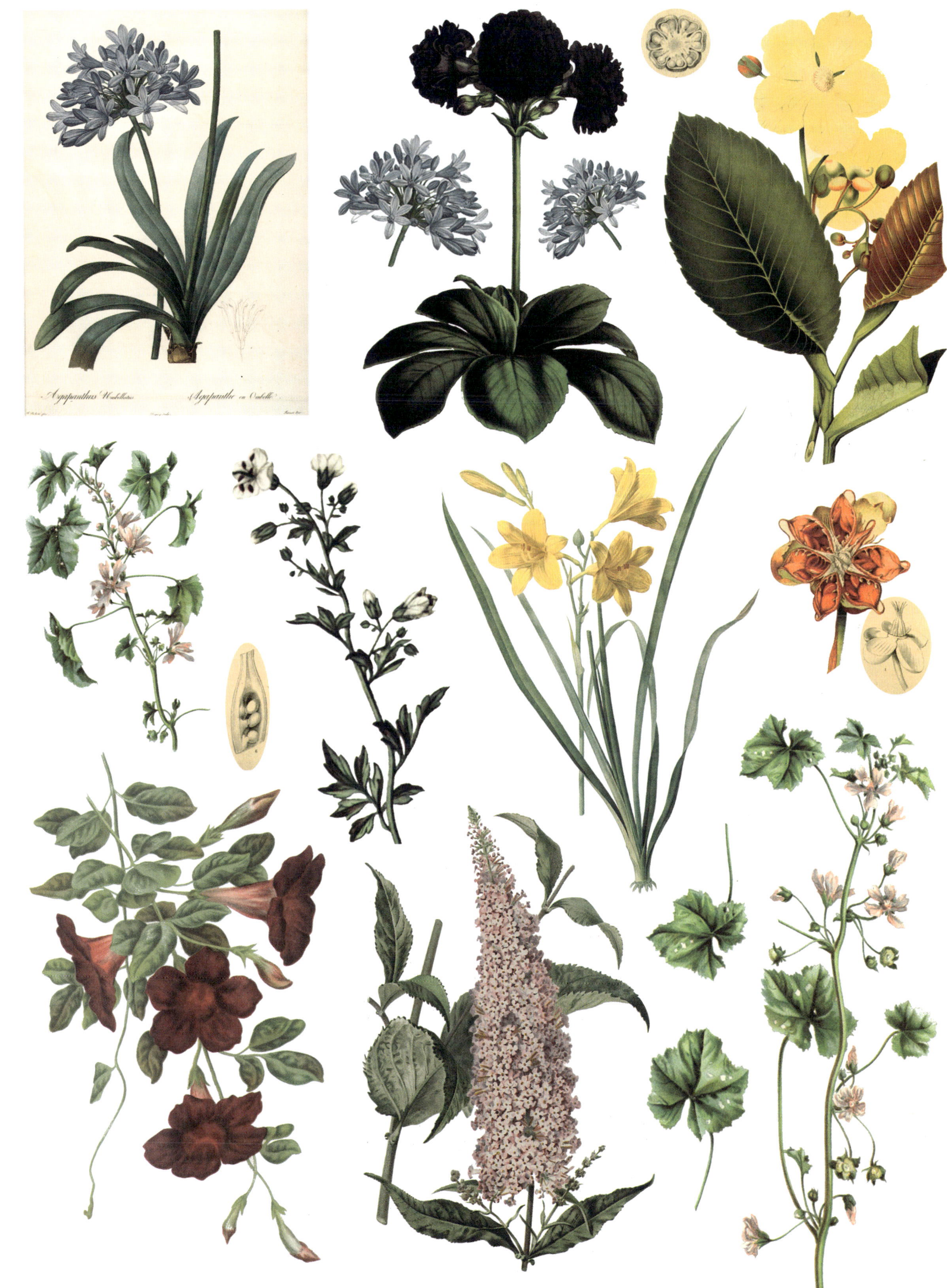
Agapanthus Umbellatus
Agapanthe en Ombelle

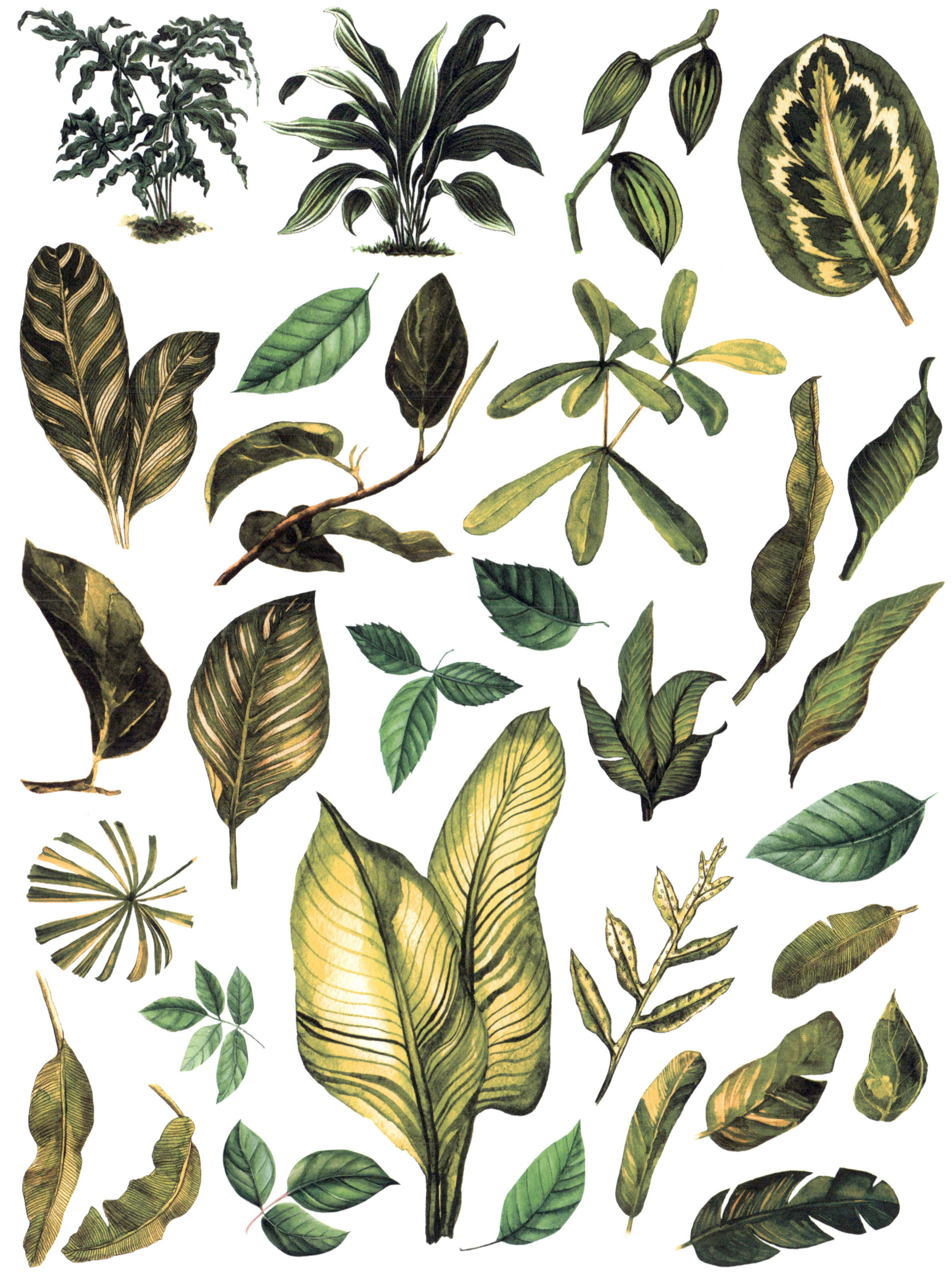

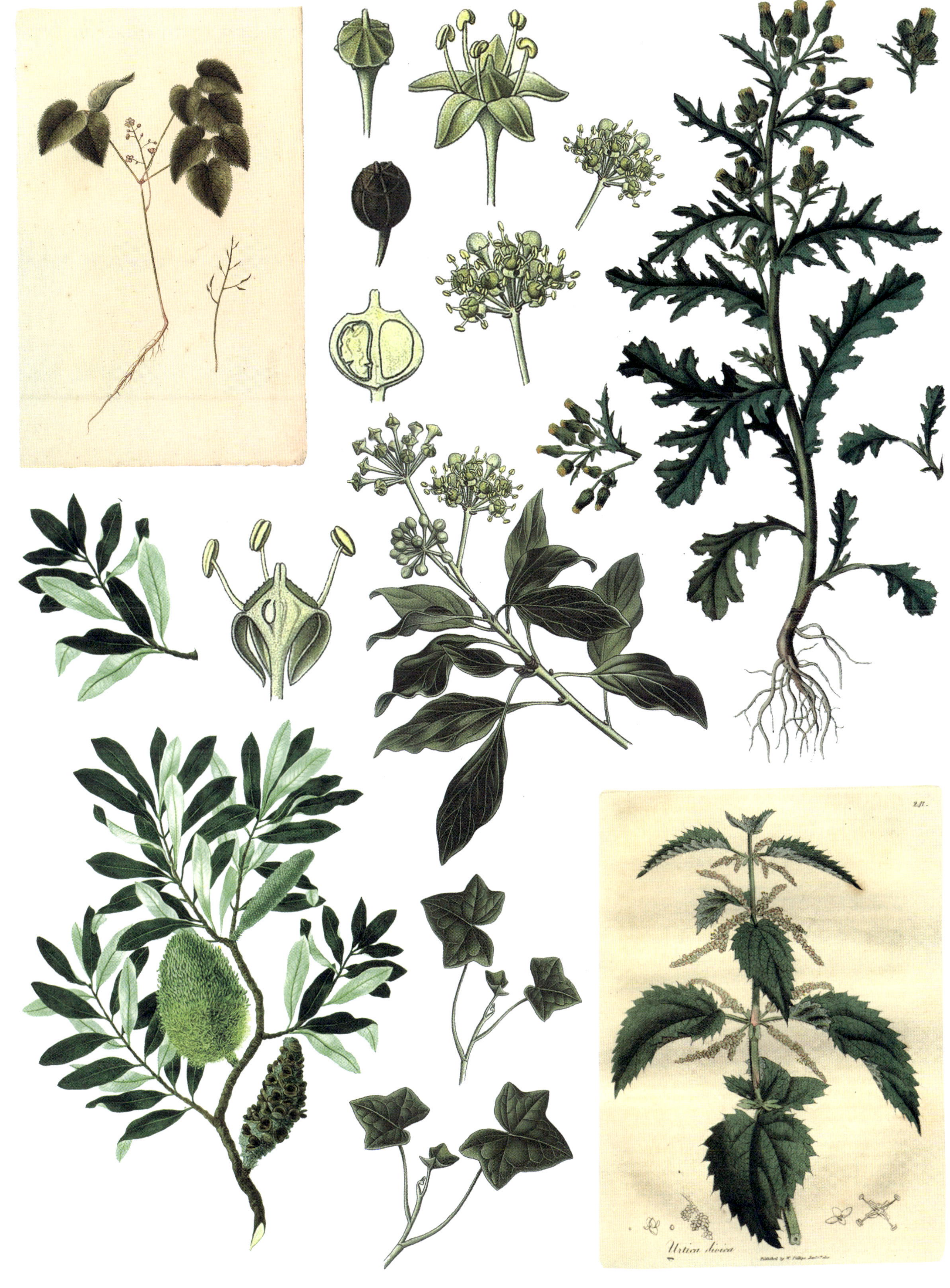
Urtica dioica

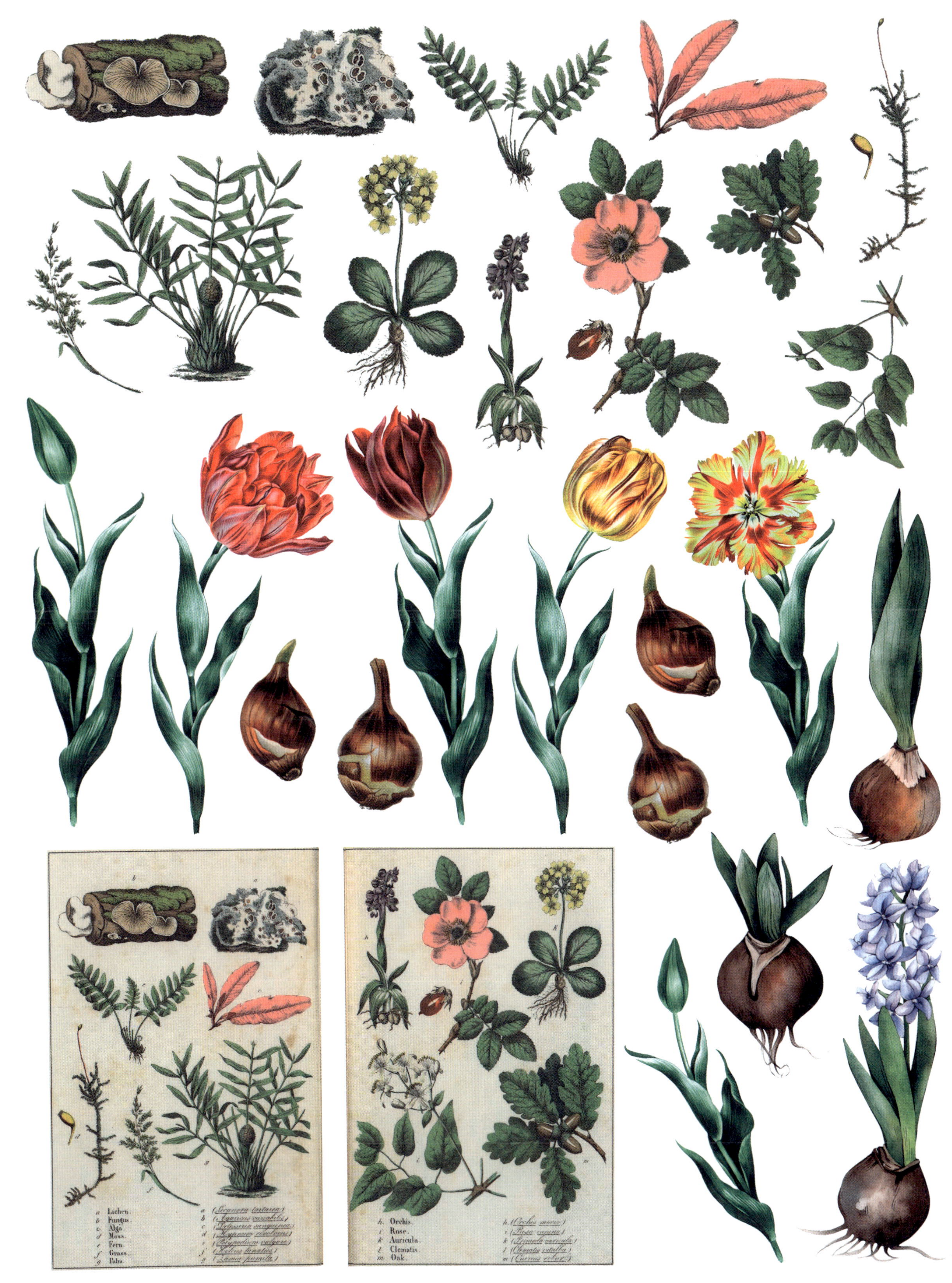

a Lichen.
b Fungus.
c Alga.
d Moss.
e Fern.
f Grass.
g Palm.
h. Orchis.
i Rose.
k Auricula.
l. Clematis.
m Oak.